The Gardened Soul

The Gardened Soul

The Emotional Connection to More

David White

FOREWORD BY
Cathriona Russell

WIPF & STOCK · Eugene, Oregon

THE GARDENED SOUL
The Emotional Connection to More

Wipf & Stock
An Imprint of Wipf and Stock Publishers
199 W. 8th Ave., Suite 3
Eugene, OR 97401

www.wipfandstock.com

PAPERBACK ISBN: 979-8-3852-4719-6
HARDCOVER ISBN: 979-8-3852-4720-2
EBOOK ISBN: 979-8-3852-4721-9

VERSION NUMBER 07/28/25

For John

Contents

Our help is in the name of the Lord,
who made heaven and earth.

Ps 124:8

Foreword

Professor Cathriona Russell
School of Religion, Theology, and Peace Studies
Trinity College, Dublin

Gardens are a complex of purposeful arrangements of natural physical objects, but their form is not fully accounted for by purely practical considerations.[1] In the recent history of the philosophy of gardens, the questions often debated first are "What counts as a garden?" and "Why do we garden?" Are gardens intensified nature or a work of art?

Jacopo Bonfadio wrote in 1541 to a fellow humanist that gardens make a "third nature, which I would not know how to name."[2] "Third" nature because in the ancient world, according to Cicero's formulation, first nature is the realm of the gods, and second nature is agriculture, the production of food and fiber to meet human needs. Gardens, as *terza natura*, are a unique confluence of art and nature in horticulture; they are expressions of human creativity beyond the necessities of labor, part of the imaginative work of memorializing and of social action. And in this meeting of *techné* and *poiesis*, gardening transforms ideas into enduring structures, as architecture can do.

1. Cooper, *Philosophy of Gardens*, 13.
2. Beck, "Third Nature," 327, 329.

Gardening as a redescription of the world can also provide a milieu, the luminous clearing, where we can consider why we would choose one path over another, and what our duties are.[3] It can be a place of moral instruction, also offering beauty, delicacy, and grandeur.

In environmental philosophy we could say that gardening is akin to "ecosystem building," not a gesture against the wild but a place where biodiversity is sustained and even extended and certainly celebrated, not silenced. It is impossible to deny the bleak horizon that is the sixth mass extinction, which on current trajectories will mean that one-third of animal and plant species will face extinction by 2050, and 70 percent by the end of the century. And gardeners, too, scrabble to save what can be saved, and often in nonlinear roundabout ways. The gardener's horizon is immediate and simultaneously long-term; it warrants an attitude that might be loosely described as "intuitive aesthetic" and a temperament for delayed fulfillment, but is never far from the "tiny envelope, infinitely old and fragile, woven by the intermingling of living things, and which we must learn to care for so that is does not disappear altogether."[4]

David White's work weaves these questions together, not in overly abstract ways but from the midst of life as a long-standing gardener and rector in the Church of Ireland. And because so much of what we experience and do as gardeners is truly ineffable and ungraspable, he deploys the word "more" in an intriguingly unspecific way, at least to begin with. Now, in any garden "more" is not always obviously better or helpful. More chaos and more spontaneous destruction can also be alarming: pigeons gnawing, seedlings damping off, old favorites thrown over in a storm or succumbed to disease. However, David suggests that all of these occurrences are also experiences of resacralization in that they are simultaneously embodied, time bound, receptive, and sapiential. He is exactly right to suggest that envisaging gardening as "battling nature" is laughable. Laughable not least because gardens are more uncovered than

3. Utsler, *Paul Ricoeur*, 75.

4. Latour, "Ecological Mutation," 27.

contrived, things rarely turn out as expected; and a sense of the comical and absurd, if not a prerequisite, is an inevitable outcome sooner or later. The garden is often gardening you!

And notions of control soon give way to more immediate matters, such as evaluating the quality of the soil, the virtues of the aspect, the cycle of seasons, future possibilities, patience, and anticipated joy. David recognizes, as many plant people do, that we all eventually follow in the path of those "reformed landscape gardeners" who realize the folly of perfection in design and repent at their leisure.

Our theological traditions too are full of gardeners in symbolic relation. Gardens are central in biblical scene-setting: God walks in the cool of the garden in Genesis, Jesus suffers agonies at Gethsemane, and most intriguingly of all, the joy of the empty tomb, where Mary Magdalene takes the risen Christ to be the gardener. Significant events unfold in the intimacy of the enclosed garden, not least the hope of paradise.

All of these sensibilities are woven into this text, and at the center of it is an affective sensibility that gardening is a practiced place and a place of departure, one that mediates between the oppositions that define people.[5] It gets us into the same room with others; we become entangled. It is at the same time a disciplined knowing, an expression of the art of paying attention. There is the wonderful ambiguity that is rarely put into words by gardeners—an emotional geography, the rhythms of the year, the rest and activity, always changing and always becoming, and the giddy playfulness of a flower—that allows us to endure and not fall into nothingness.

And from this point of departure, David presents us with two interior landscapes that connect to the "more." The first is that love is expressed in the practice of gratitude; the garden is no longer a place to be looked at or labored over only, but a place for living. The second is that there, in that luminous clearing, is a place for lament where, unhurried, sadness can hope to be transformed into

5. Cooper, *Philosophy of Gardens*, 4.

the practice of everyday joy. Where joy, always a tricky customer, becomes the good mood of the soul.

In introducing us to the gardened soul, David reconnects us to creation and to a profoundly rooted version of contemplation, one that rematerializes, as Bruno Latour expresses it, "the thousand different ways of our belonging to the Earth" played out in the terrestrial here.[6]

6. Latour, "Ecological Mutation," v.

Acknowledgments

The year completing the MA in applied spirituality at South East Technological University (SETU) was a time of learning and nurturing, affirmation and challenge. Above every other emotion, I was left with a sense of gratitude. I would like to extend my thanks to the following:

My classmates for being part of a journey of transformation where we all felt cherished.

Dr. Noelia Molina, Dr. Bernadette Flanagan, and Dr. Michael O'Sullivan for their encouragement, commitment, and warm humanity.

The other members of staff, and those who volunteer, for sharing so generously.

Sr. Kathleen Lyng in the SpIRE Library for her gentle attentiveness.

Dr. Bernadette Masterson, my spiritual director, for her companionship, wisdom, and sense of fun.

Dr. Elizabeth McCrory, my research supervisor, for her support, guidance, and insight.

Professor Cathriona Russell for writing the foreword and for her inspiration over many years. And to those who so generously agreed to write endorsements.

Finally, to John, my partner in life and companion in the garden, for all that he means to me and to whom this book is dedicated.

Abstract

THIS RESEARCH WILL ADDRESS how a receptive engagement with gardening as a spiritual practice can allow for the emergence of a sacred environment, where emotions can lead the soul deeper into the experience of more, particularly into the development of other embodied spiritual practices.

Framed within the contemplative spiritual framework and employing organic inquiry as the research method, the research focuses on the garden as a "practiced place," where the garden is experienced as dynamic and relational. The garden is the particular place where, through the emotions, the soul is invited to cross the boundary into liminal space, as the soul's vibrancy flourishes through following its deepest desire.

Emotions lead to more and, in themselves, may become embodied spiritual practices. The two specific emotions examined in this study are love and sadness, which are explored as they grow into the embodied practices of gratitude and "everyday joy," respectively. Love and gratitude inspire a longing for fulfillment rooted in hopeful promises, and their cultivation in the garden leads to a deeper connection with the self and the world. Similarly, sadness, when embodied as "everyday joy," allows for empathy and receptivity to thrive, potentially on a daily basis.

Our help is in the name of the Lord,
who made heaven and earth.

Ps 124:8

Introduction

DURING THE FIRST LOCKDOWN of the Covid pandemic, I spent the morning writing and catching up on administration work in the parish. Every day the weather was sunny and warm. So, in the afternoon I was in the garden. As I was cutting back some shrubs, I had a strong feeling of gratitude for being able to spend the afternoons gardening. The thought was, "Isn't it great to be able to garden?" This was quickly followed by a second thought, "But isn't it the garden that's gardening you?"

Seeing the garden as more than a piece of land to grow plants means that we open ourselves up to the possibility that we are being gardened and also being led to an experience of more. This experience of more will differ from person to person. But what may be held in common is that it will be an invitation, and perhaps even a challenge, to something life-giving and transformative. For example, when biblical gardens are considered, they may be understood as archetypal for all gardens that have been created, since all gardens are places where earth and soul intertwine, and where the result is always a yearning for more.

This research will address how a receptive engagement with gardening as a spiritual practice can allow for the emergence of a sacred environment where emotions can lead the soul deeper into the experience of more, particularly into the development of embodied spiritual practices. The research takes place within the contemplative spiritual framework so that the garden is viewed as the contemplative locus for seeking more, where the emotions can add to the depth of vision and the increase of insight for the soul. The contemplative lens helps us to avoid the temptation to dualize and instead leads to a more integrated vision of the self and all that makes up our experience of life.

Through the process of organic inquiry (OI), within the contemplative spiritual framework, the research seeks to encourage an openness to the possibility of the garden being a locus for embodied spiritual practice where the soul may be cultivated and nourished. OI puts personal experience at the heart of the process, so this method is ideally suited to topics related to psycho-spiritual growth. While the role of the researcher's experience is vital in this method, subjectivity and reflexivity must be balanced with objectivity and concerns for validity.

While gardens have played a significant role in religious and spiritual traditions, symbolizing hope, transformation, and our connection with the divine, what if they were also spaces for intentional spiritual practice? The research will show that gardens may be described as "spaces" in the sense that Michel de Certeau means by his term "practiced places."[1] They especially become dynamic and relational when they are used for embodied praxis where the soul can be nourished. When we garden the soul, we do so as embodied emotional beings, since the soul must always have a form. Therefore, practices can give shape to the desire for more, supported by the practiced place of the garden so that the emotions nourish and challenge the soul which continues to journey and develop. Gardening is not just about cultivating plants. It is also about tending to the soul, a means of contemplatively engaging with core questions, and exploring the interrelationship between humans and nature.

Emotions lead to more and in themselves may become embodied spiritual practices. The emotions which will be considered are *love* as it grows into the embodied practice of gratitude and *sadness* as it grows into the embodied practice of, what this researcher has termed, "everyday joy."

1. De Certeau, *Practice of Everyday Life*, 117.

When we listen out for the melody of love, the response grows into the embodiment of gratitude as a practice. Love and gratitude inspire a hopeful longing for our destiny which is rooted in both. When love is threatened, the challenge is to keep the promise of love before us so that we can make room for feelings of gratitude. When love is cultivated, it becomes contagious and takes root in our thankful souls. Love and the embodied practice of gratitude lead us to more.

Sadness has the capacity to draw us out of our interior garden so that empathy is met with receptivity, and both can blossom in the garden of relationship and collaboration. When sadness grows into "everyday joy" and is embodied, it becomes the background music of the soul. The emotional experience can be one of wonder and excitement as something yet unfurled is noticed and loved into life. Sadness and the embodied practice of "everyday joy" lead us to more.

Chapter One: **The Ground of the Research**

1.1 Introduction

THE CONCEPT OF GARDENING transcends a narrow definition that only recognizes it as the act of creating a space for cultivating plants. Gardening is much more than that. The experience of people for millennia suggests that gardens are places where the soul is gardened as much as the soil is cultivated. A contemplative engagement with the emotions is key to the deepening of this experience so that there is room for the soul to grow. The open space of a garden then, may reflect the nature of the soul which, as Teresa of Avila puts it, is "spacious, plentiful, and its amplitude is impossible to exaggerate. . . . The sun here radiates to every part . . . and nothing can diminish its beauty."[1] Gardens serve as gateways into the profound beauty and abundance that lies deep within us. The challenge then, as Jeremy Naydler sees it, is to "re-sacralise our work as gardeners," to "work at re-sensitising ourselves" to the presence of God in the natural world "so that our gardens may come to feel more and more like icons, mediating that which is numinous in nature."[2]

1. Rohr, *Immortal Diamond*, 23.
2. Naydler, *Gardening*, 98.

To complete this review, a literature search was carried out using multiple online search engines including Google Books and Google Scholar. The databases accessed included JSTOR, Web of Science, and PubMed. However, since there are limited available journal articles relevant to this area, in the main, printed resources from my personal collection and from SpIRE (Spirituality Institute for Research and Education), RCB (Representative Church Body), and SETU (South East Technological University) libraries were accessed.

This review of the relevant literature will establish the ground of the research, firstly by addressing the questions "Why garden?" and "What is a garden?" Then it will explore some archetypal gardens, followed by the relationship between gardening and health. The interaction between gardening, nature, and healing will be considered, and afterwards, there will be an examination of the role that emotions have in gardening. Finally, the question "How does gardening have its effects on us?" will be addressed.

1.2 "Why Garden?"

For some, gardening is a tiresome kind of outdoor housework. Yet for others, like Dan O'Brien, gardening is "a human activity that engages with core philosophical questions, concerning, among other things, human well-being, wisdom, the nature of time, political power and ideals, home, aesthetic experience, metaphysics, and religion."[3]

Engaging in the planning, growth, and cultivation of a garden extends beyond simply producing flowers or vegetables or creating a pleasant outdoor space. Instead, it taps into the essence of being a human, allowing individuals to derive meaning from their personal experience. But the Japanese garden designer Marc Keane asks a fundamental question, "Why garden?"[4] The answers to this question will be as numerous as the people who engage

3. O'Brien, *Gardening*, 1.

4. Keane, *Japanese Garden Design*, 118.

in gardening. But it could be argued that the garden is not just simply an outside room but is a realm for spiritual exploration, whatever this may mean to the individual gardener. However, as David Cooper insightfully stresses, "The significance that the garden has for people need not, of course, be something that they are able easily, or even at all, to spell out."[5]

1.3 "What Is a Garden?"

This begs another question, "What is a garden?" Since people began gardening back in the mists of time, there have been so many styles of design, different aspects of emphasis, and also uses of these outdoor environments.[6] But all gardens differ from wild landscapes that have not been interfered with by humans. So gardens could be defined, as Gordon Campell puts it, as

> a planned outdoor space distinguished from its surroundings by either a formal enclosure or a marked stylistic difference. . . . The design of the garden reflects its purposes, which may be recreational, aesthetic, practical, or contemplative.[7]

Seeing the garden as more than a piece of land to grow plants means that, as Campbell claims, "at a deeper level, the garden represents the interdependence of humans and other parts of the natural world. The garden is a space designated for a partnership between human activity and a compliant natural world."[8] From this perspective, the garden is a place of communion where the gardener and the garden are in a symbiotic relationship where both have the potential to thrive. On the other hand, Mara Miller makes the case that gardening, rather than being unitive and contemplative, "mediates" between several "oppositions that define

5. Cooper, *Philosophy of Gardens*, 4.
6. Bowe and Lamb, *History of Gardening in Ireland.*
7. Campbell, *Garden History*, 1.
8. Campbell, *Garden History*, 2.

human experience" such as "man and nature" and "action and contemplation."[9]

1.4 Archetypal Gardens

In the Judeo-Christian tradition, gardens have been places where fundamental aspects of our identity have been explored. From the garden of Eden (Gen 2:8) to the garden of the resurrection (John 19:41), the drama of the people of God, the experience of individual seekers, and God's desire for all that God had made, have all been played out in these outdoor spaces.

Paul Morris writing about the Genesis story remarks that "our primary relationships—between man and woman, humanity and deity, and humanity and nature—have been defined by our understanding of this biblical text." And that "the Garden narrative has been central in informing both the meaning and content of our sexual, moral, artistic and literary traditions."[10] The story of the garden of Eden is a living part of our anthropology.

From the perspective of the Christian Scriptures, Arthur Roche uses the language of emotion when he explores the sorrow of Gethsemane, the joy of the empty tomb, the intimacy of the enclosed garden, and the hope of paradise.[11] The gardens found in these Scriptures are the locus for searching and grappling for something more. In the garden of Eden, our connection with God was compromised and the complex nature of our humanity was revealed. In the garden of the resurrection, hope grew out of the devastation of the cross. Yet in this place of hope and transformation, Mary Magdalene could not see who was right in front of her eyes and presumed that the resurrected Christ was the gardener (John 20:15).[12] Her journey of faith, like ours, is complex and complicated and truly will not cease until we take our last breath.

9. Miller, *Garden as Art*, 57.

10. Morris and Sawyer, *Walk in the Garden*, 21.

11. Roche, *Gardens of God*.

12. Daly-Denton, *John*.

Both gardens are archetypal for all gardens that have been created since all gardens are places where earth and soul intertwine, and the result is always a yearning for more.

1.5 Gardening and Health

The twelfth-century mystic Hildegard von Bingen knew about the link between nature and human health and called the power in plants and all living beings "greening power."[13] In Ireland, a largely rural people through indigenous wisdom gathered an abundance of knowledge about plants and their benefits to health. Niall Mac Coitir notes this closeness to the natural world when he writes, "Wild plants appear in the ancient Irish Behon Laws and in early nature poetry. . . . Herbal medicine was important too in Ireland. For instance, it was believed that there were 365 parts of the body, and that a different wild herb existed to cure the ills of each part."[14]

There is also a considerable body of contemporary research that suggests that gardening is good for our health.[15] Being outdoors in natural light, physical exercise and a sense of achievement and connection contribute to our sense of well-being. Some research also suggests that we not only depend on nature for our physical needs but also our emotional needs.[16] The medical doctor Esther Sternberg writing about gardens, the connection with place and the emotional response to both, points out that "each of these emotions triggers cascades of nerve chemicals and hormones, which are released through the outflow pathways of the brain."[17] Being in the garden touches the deepest processes of our being. Research has also shown that people often describe their personal relationship with the natural environment using phrases like communing with

13. Arvay, *Biophilia Effect*, 5.

14. Mac Coitir, *Ireland's Wild Plants*, 2.

15. Soga et al., "Gardening Is Beneficial." See also Koay and Dillon, "Community Gardening"; and Bell-Williams et al., "Digging Deeper."

16. Davis et al., "Interdependence with the Environment."

17. Sternberg, *Healing Spaces*, 290.

nature, living in harmony with the environment, and feeling a personal connection to the natural world and its future. "These phrases are borrowed," Davis, Green, and Reed claim, "from language usually used to describe interpersonal bonds."[18]

1.6 Gardens, Nature, and Healing

Mary Reynolds describes herself as a "reformed garden designer." She realized that in her work of creating garden designs, she was failing to work in harmony with nature. She makes the point that "the words 'garden' and 'nature' have become almost synonymous, but in reality they have very little in common any more."[19] Through reexamining her approach, she discovered that she needed to "invite Nature to express her true self in these spaces and then work to heal the land and bring it back into balance."[20] This careful balancing between human engagement with the land and what the land needs of us is core to her philosophy.

> We are only brief guardians of these portions of land we call our gardens. We do not and cannot truly own them. Our bodies are made of the Earth and return to it eventually, but the land will always remain alive. . . . We are simply walking pieces of earth.[21]

Mary Reynolds lives and works in a manner that embodies the belief that nature is our true home. This closeness has been described as "the biophilia hypothesis"[22] since, as John Feehan claims, "human beings evolved as creatures deeply enmeshed with the intricacies of nature, and . . . we still have this affinity with nature ingrained in our genotype."[23] This is the place of our true belonging. But how we engage with nature will say much

18. Davis et al., "Interdependence with the Environment."
19. Reynolds, *Garden Awakening*, 13.
20. Reynolds, *Garden Awakening*, 13–14.
21. Reynolds, *Garden Awakening*, 19.
22. Arvay, *Biophilia Effect*, 2.
23. Feehan, *Singing Heart of the World*, 174–75.

about how we understand this relationship. The garden ought to be a place of interdependence and mutual respect. When Robin Wall Kimmerer is asked about how to restore the relationship between land and people, her answer draws on her Potawatomi heritage. "Plant a garden," she says. "It's good for the health of the earth and it's good for the health of people."[24] Through gardening, we demonstrate that the needs of the garden are as important as those of the gardener and that positive engagement has the potential to be mutually beneficial.

1.7 Gardens and Emotions

"Throughout history," Anita Phillips contends, "people of many religions have sought spiritual insight amongst seeds, soil, plants, and fruit."[25] The garden for her is the place where she can find answers to many of the greatest questions of life through an engagement with the emotions and a close reading of the Scriptures. From her experience as a pastor and trauma therapist, she writes,

> A garden's condition depends on its soil; the condition of the garden within you—spiritually, mentally, and physically—depends on the soil of your heart. That means embracing your feelings. All of them. And that means it's time to end the war.[26]

We must shed this battlefield mentality when it comes to our emotions. Instead, we are invited to integration so that our emotions are embodied.[27] For "it is only our *unattended* sadness, anger, and fear that eventually threaten the ground of our hearts, not the feeling itself."[28] At the heart of her message is that "the first step to living a powerful life is to commit to cultivating a state of emotional well-being that will catalyze, sustain, and

24. Wall Kimmerer, *Braiding Sweetgrass*, 126.
25. Phillips, *Garden Within*, 1.
26. Phillips, *Garden Within*, 13.
27. Phillips, *Garden Within*, 94–95.
28. Phillips, *Garden Within*, 21; emphasis is original.

nourish what we choose to plant."[29] Intriguingly she is not an "avid gardener" but draws great inspiration and insight from her reflection on plants and how they grow.[30]

1.8 "How Does Gardening Have Its Effects on Us?"

The psychotherapist and psychiatrist Sue Stuart-Smith gardens along with her husband, Tom, in Hertfordshire. She uses a combination of contemporary neuroscience, psychoanalysis, and compelling real-life stories to express her contention that the garden can prove a vital place to cultivate the mind. She writes, "I have come to understand that deep existential processes can be involved in creating and caring for a garden. So I find myself asking, How does gardening have its effects on us?"[31] Recognizing that gardens have been seen as restorative from ancient times, she also sees important roles for gardens today:

> Ancient because of the evolutionary fit between brain and nature, and also ancient as the way of life between foraging and farming, that expresses our deeply inscribed need to attach the place. Modern, because the garden is intrinsically forward-looking and the gardeners always aiming for a better future.[32]

In today's world, she sees an urgent need for a return to the nature of reality as can be experienced through the natural world. This requires humility, openness, and the courage to learn from the garden.

> Cultivation works both ways; it is inward as well as outward and tending a garden can become an attitude towards life. In a world that is increasingly dominated by technology and consumption, gardening puts us in a direct relationship with the reality of how life is generated and sustained, and with how fragile and fleeting it can be

29. Phillips, *Garden Within*, 28.
30. Phillips, *Garden Within*, 5.
31. Stuart-Smith, *Well Gardened Mind*, 13.
32. Stuart-Smith, *Well Gardened Mind*, 285–86.

> now, more than ever, we need to remind ourselves that first and foremost we are creatures of the earth.[33]

1.9 Conclusion

Gardening is not just about cultivating plants. It is also about tending to the soul as a means of contemplatively engaging with core questions and exploring the interrelationship between humans and nature. Gardens have played a significant role in religious and spiritual traditions, symbolizing hope, transformation, and our connection with the divine. "Gardens have given people a place of respite since the beginning of recorded history," remarks Esther Sternberg, "and in legend, poetry and song: the Garden of Eden, the hanging gardens of Babylon, the gardens along the ancient Silk Road of Persia, India, China, and Japan."[34] Contemporary research also suggests that gardening is beneficial for our overall well-being, both physically and emotionally. The study of the role of emotions has benefitted from the research of people like Brené Brown.[35]

However, this review of the relevant literature has discovered that the relationship between gardens and spirituality has not been as fully explored as it might be. Gardening allows us to commune with nature and cultivate a state of emotional well-being, and this is worthy of more research, contemplative engagement, and scholarly attention. Therefore, this research, which is concerned with how a receptive engagement with gardening as a spiritual practice allows for the emergence of a sacred environment where emotions can lead the soul deeper into the experience of more, seems apposite and timely. The act of gardening, after all, can have profound effects on our minds and souls and can serve as a reminder of our intrinsic connection to the earth. Ultimately, people garden for various reasons, but it is always driven by a desire for something more.

33. Stuart-Smith, *Well Gardened Mind*, 286.

34. Sternberg, *Healing Spaces*, 283.

35. Brown, *Atlas of the Heart*.

Chapter Two: **Spirituality Through Contemplation**

2.1 Introduction

Contemplation is a spiritual framework which creates an environment where there is "an intensification of a transforming awareness of divine presence"[1] along with a growing desire for greater intimacy with this same God. Since there is something of God in all things,[2] contemplation can also be described as the desire for a connection to more: more unity between inner and outer worlds as described by Kerrie Hide, more recognition of how the researcher's own story resonates within the study of spirituality as articulated by Mary Frohlich, a personal seeking of integration by this researcher, how ordinary things can contain a world of connection to more in the vision of Julian of Norwich, geography allowing a "third space" for the emotions to deepen contemplation, and the garden providing the ideal locus of seeking for more as seen through Franz Jalics's contemplation on a little flower.

This chapter will first explore Kerry Hide's phrase "one verse of love" and then analyze Mary Frohlich's development of the contemplative method. Following this, there is a personal reflection on seeking integration through contemplation, and then

1. Egan, "Contemplation," 211.

2. Hughes, *God in All Things*, 50.

Julian of Norwich's meditation on a hazelnut will be explored. The relationship between geography, emotions, and the garden will then be examined. The chapter ends with Franz Jalics's contemplation of a little flower.

2.2 Kerrie Hide: "One Verse of Love"

The Franciscan theologian Ilia Delio reminds us that there is a profound need today "to recover the mystical dimension of life beginning in the human heart as that heart extends into the cosmos . . . that God-centered love that holds us together moment to moment and constantly creates us anew."[3] The journey begins within but is always propelled to union with the world without. This insight shuns any sense of dualism and opens our perspectives to the blessings and benefits of living in a state of oneness. By incarnating this unity, we honor our Maker and seek the wholeness and healing which is God's desire and gift for everything and everyone in the universe.

The mystical theologian Kerrie Hide describes this desire for more as the "unitive, or oneing consciousness" and that there is a certain "wisdom that arises from this oneing."[4] This contemplative approach allows us to find our place in the wholeness of the universe as we inhabit our bodies and souls in a spirit of open receptivity.

> We must rediscover how to enter into the ground of our heart, in the divine heart and consciously participate in the newness of the fullness of divine love evolving. This includes embodying how the inner universe and outer universe are one verse of love. I understand heart to be the centre, the luminous, spacious energy field of pure oneness, that is within our deepest interiority, extending into the cosmos.[5]

3. Delio, *Unbearable Wholeness of Being*, 182–83.
4. Hide, *Love's Oneing*, i.
5. Hide, *Love's Oneing*, iii.

Hide's phrase "one verse of love" captures well the desire at the heart of the contemplative approach to developing non-dual consciousness so that all of our existence might be spent in the oneness of contemplation which leads into the "dynamism of the intimacy of being one in God."[6]

2.3 Mary Frohlich: Interconnected, Whole, and in Harmony

Mary Frohlich describes the contemplative method as "an articulation of the innate dynamism that has shaped the cosmos and, within it, ourselves."[7] This intimate connection between the inner experience of the individual and the cosmos as a whole is at the heart of the study of spirituality. Frohlich claims that "studying spirituality is constitutively self-implicating; that is, one cannot even recognize the 'data' of our field except by awareness of how they resonate in one's own spirit."[8] She draws on the work of Francisco Varela who said that the researcher must be "an empathic resonator with experiences that are familiar to him [or her] and which find in himself [or herself] a resonant chord."[9] She suggests that while this "resonance" "does not actually put us inside another's experience, it at least gets us into the same room, so to speak. The 'room' is spiritual experience as the root of spirituality."[10] This seems to chime with Margaret Benefiel's assertion that "experience, which is necessarily subjective, is a crucial foundation of knowledge. . . . Our subjectivity enters into every aspect of our knowing."[11]

Thomas Berry uses the principles of subjectivity, differentiation, and communion to articulate the ways in which the

6. Hide, *Love's Oneing*, vi.

7. Frohlich, "Spirit," 139.

8. Frohlich, "Spirit," 133. See Frohlich, "Spiritual Discipline."

9. Varela and Shear, "First-Person Methodologies," 10; inclusive language added.

10. Frohlich, "Spirit," 133–34.

11. Benefiel, "Epistemological Foundations," 6–7.

universe is proceeding and developing and that these terms encapsulate the dynamic process at work. Frohlich goes on to build on Berry's three phases and develops a contemplative approach to method which corresponds to one of these three basic principles of cosmic process.

> Phase one, *Presence*, affirms contemplative subjectivity as our foundation.
>
> Phase two, *Search*, affirms the struggle of differentiation as the path to renewed life.
>
> Phase three, *Emergence*, affirms emergent communion as our goal.[12]

She is anxious to explain that while there are three stages in the process, "each of the three phases is actually a stance that permeates the entire process, yet emerges into more concentrated focus sequentially."[13] The method has a dynamic unity at its core which is not bound by the limiting constraints of an understanding of what is happening as sequential process. She concludes, "If we are to be scholars of the dynamism of the human spirit on its urgent journey to the fullness of life in communion with the divine Spirit and the cosmos, we cannot do so without living that contemplative journey to the full."[14]

2.4 A Personal Reflection: Seeking Integration

Every spring the blushed-pink flowers of the apple tree hold my attention. After the long dreary months of winter, they are like little signs of potentiality in the garden. After they have been pollinated by some generous bee, they will begin to form the fruit to be enjoyed in autumn. But this marvelous festival of nature goes deeper than mere biology, as it deepens my sense of wonder and increases my desire to be one with nature. Year after year, this yearning

12. Frohlich, "Spirit," 138; emphasis is original.

13. Frohlich, "Spirit," 138.

14. Frohlich, "Spirit," 139.

never diminishes but is like a thirst that is never fully quenched. Contemplating in the garden always leads to an invitation which is always to more. An entry in my journal captures the essence of this seeking beyond the obvious, to a place where there is no separation between our inner and outer worlds.

> The garden can never be static as its great work goes on with an unrushed hum. The flowers attract their pollinators; earthworms enrich the soil; and leaves bend to catch the sunlight. An unheard beat accompanies the unfolding of nature unselfconsciously being itself. There is no forcing here, for surely that would go against the flow of life. All is unrushed and unharried as the garden breathes deeply in its own spaciousness. With every clunk of the spade, the garden's rhythm soothes the gardener's furrowed brow. The ease of growth reminds us that much of our pain is about things that will never happen. Wrongly imagined futures sit alone on some foreign horizon. Allowing our bodies to speak distracts from the false busyness of our minds. And there is no better place on a dewy morning than the garden to dig and clip and above all savor. The garden teaches us so much if we listen with our arms and legs rather than being lost in our internal monotony. The sheer diversity of life infuses our lifeblood with possibility and the desire to feel and be more. When we have ears to hear, futures open up for us which are infused with color and the vibrancy of longing.

2.5 Julian of Norwich: "What Is This?"

Through the simple fruit of the hazel tree, the medieval contemplative Julian of Norwich senses inklings of a deeper reality, an invitation to more. Holding a hazelnut in the open palm of her hand, she focuses her attention while being drawn to question, "What is this?" The result is that she transcends its small, understated, and apparent ordinariness as her vision is expanded and her consciousness is immersed with wonder and insight. There is a resonance here with the Irish tradition which holds stories of sacred fish which had eaten the *cuil crimaind* or the magical hazelnuts that gave the fish wisdom.[15] These hazelnuts are, according to Manchán Magan, always "a metaphor for gaining enlightenment."[16] Ellyn Sanna tells the story of this episode in Julian's life in contemporary language:

> At the same time, the Spirit showed me a tiny thing the size of a hazelnut, as round as a ball and so small I could hold it in the palm of my hand. I looked at it in my mind's eye and wondered, "What is this?" The answer came to me: "This is everything that has been made. This is all Creation." It was so small that I marvelled it could endure; such a tiny thing seemed likely to simply fall into nothingness. Again the answer came to thoughts: "It lasts, and it will always last, because God loves it." Everything—all that exists—draws its being from God's love.[17]

Julian realized in that moment the truth of the interconnectedness of all things, and that the fragmentation of the whole is an illusion. God was present and active in all things such as a "blade of grass, a cloud, a drop of water, a rock, a tree, a flower, a bird, a fish, an animal, each and every human being."[18] Yet in this experience she remains restless and desires more insight. She is being invited to more. As Veronica Mary Rolf puts it, "Still, she is not satisfied."[19]

2.6 Emotional Geography and the Garden

The garden provides the contemplative locus for seeking more where the emotions can give depth and more insight to our lived experience. "Emotional geography" has become an area of study over recent years, and Martin Jordan claims that this approach "attempts to understand emotion as experiential and conceptual, and how it is mediated and articulated in a social-spatial way

15. Magan, *Listen to the Land Speak*, 41. See Murray, *Wild Embrace*, 180.
16. Magan, *Listen to the Land Speak*, 41.
17. Sanna, *All Shall Be Well*, 36.
18. Sanna, *All Shall Be Well*, 73.
19. Rolf, *Julian of Norwich*, 73.

rather than as a purely interiorized subjective mental state."[20] In other words, emotions are situated spatially in that "different geographic spaces have an effect on emotions and that different outdoor locations can have an effect on feelings." Considering a therapeutic context, with a therapist and client dyad, he suggests that nature acts as a "third space."[21] The garden can act as an outdoor space where the inner life can be explored.

The contemplative lens helps to avoid the temptation to dualize and instead leads to a more integrated vision of the self. Arthur Versluis, from his own experience, claims that "for the contemplative spirit, wildness is crucial. We draw sustenance from nature; we are perpetually renewed by it."[22] This renewal will be more fruitful when we engage with the natural world in an open and unguarded way since "the contemplative life is far easier and more powerful if it is woven into the fabric of a life lived close to the land, close to rhythms of the year, the falling snow, the spring rivulets, the summer haze, the autumn sunlight against the colourful leaves."[23]

2.7 Franz Jalics: A Little Flower

"Meaningful experience is pretty much impossible without metaphor," writes Blake Parker, since "it's clear that part of all our experience as sentient human beings is the perception of metaphoric meaning."[24] Much of our meaning-making is through image, language, and the immediate felt experience. The contemplative approach challenges us, however, to go beyond what is habitual into the field of the uncomfortable and perhaps even the unknown. We then come face-to-face with the reality of our incompleteness and unwillingness to transcend our limited horizons. "My problem is one of limited imagination," Belden Lane

20. Jordan, "Ecotherapy as Psychotherapy," 63.
21. Jordan, "Ecotherapy as Psychotherapy," 67.
22. Versluis, *Awakening the Contemplative Spirit*, 79.
23. Versluis, *Awakening the Contemplative Spirit*, 79.
24. Parker, *Forest of Ideas*, 19.

shares. "Like most of us, I simply can't believe that God's love is actually as exuberant and playful as it is."[25]

When Franz Jalics contemplated a little flower, he allowed playfulness to guide his imagination so that he went beyond the physical into an expansive realm. The little flower, he wrote, is "a little flame" that is "meant to become a mighty fire."[26]

> The new life begins like the flower. Just watch closely how it grows: at first you hardly notice how the tip of the blade, bit by bit, slowly creeps out of the soil, but it doesn't take long till the flower is in full bloom - all by itself! We only have to keep our eyes wide open and observe closely where a new life is in the making. The new little flower wants to grow. And we, for our part, have to protect it, foster its growth, and take care to see that enough sun and rain reach it and that it isn't damaged.[27]

The potential of the contemplative approach can easily be diminished by cynical materialism where all sense of wonder is replaced by life-denying utilitarianism. Brian Swimme was able to hold serious science and fun together when he said, "This is the greatest discovery of the scientific enterprise: You take hydrogen gas, and you leave it alone, and it turns into rosebushes, giraffes, and humans."[28] Contemplation always leads us to see and experience more.

2.8 Conclusion

Contemplation is a spiritual framework that increases vision, and depth of experience, and challenges any attempt to make the human soul small. Richard Rohr lamented that "we are a circumference people, with little access to the center."[29] The contemplative approach leads us towards what is essential, to what is central, so

25. Lane, *Solace of Fierce Landscapes*, 182.
26. Jalics, *Contemplative Way*, 73.
27. Jalics, *Contemplative Way*, 73.
28. Bridle, "Comprehensive Compassion."
29. Rohr, *Everything Belongs*, 13.

that our souls can feast on what is whole and holy and in turn be transformed. Douglas Christie writes about "the fragmentation and alienation that haunts existence at the deepest possible level" but suggests that "through sustained practice" we can "come to realize a different, more integrated way of being in the world" as "the contemplative seeks to recover a vision of the whole and a new way of living in relationship to the whole."[30] Contemplation as a spiritual framework resonates with this research, which is concerned with how a receptive engagement with gardening as a spiritual practice allows for the emergence of a sacred environment where emotions can lead the soul deeper into the experience of more.

30. Christie, *Blue Sapphire*, 36.

Chapter Three: **An Organic Inquiry**

3.1 Introduction

This research project uses the organic inquiry (OI) method within the contemplative spiritual framework. OI holds that all things are interconnected, and through deep spiritual engagement, the researcher may come into contact with more, leading to transformation in learning and of heart and soul. Gardening is used as a metaphor where the seed of the researcher's experience grows and expands into a fruit tree. With its origins around 1994, it draws on the work of Jennifer Clements, Dorothy Ettling, Dianne Jennett, and Lisa Shields, among others. It has its roots in transpersonal and feminist methodologies that are exploratory and discovery oriented.[1]

The original five principles of the model—sacred, personal, chthonic, related, and transformative—are to be seen, as Jennifer Clements puts it, as "cumulative rather than successive."[2] Deah Curry and Steven Wells add a sixth principle, the numinous.[3] There is also a three-step process of preparation, inspiration, and integration that

1. Clements et al., *Organic Inquiry*.
2. Clements, "Organic Inquiry," 30.
3. Curry and Wells, *Organic Inquiry Primer*, 9–10.

governs both data collection and analysis and which leads into the liminal realm. (See diagram on page 23.)

This chapter will explore the six principles of the model and then the three steps of the process of engaging with data. A short discussion of some limitations of this method will follow. Finally, the sources of data used in this research will be identified followed by an explanation of why this particular method has been chosen.

3.2 Six-Step Process of Organic Inquiry

3.2.1 The Sacred

Planting a garden involves creating the correct conditions for the plants to flourish. The same is true when it comes to OI in that a sacred environment must be developed where ideas, thoughts, and experiences can be allowed to take root in the developing process of research. "We define the term *the sacred* as an attitude or atmosphere in which one is aware of, and respectful and reverential toward, the indwelling of Spirit," explains Deah Curry and Steven Wells, "which we distinguish as the living energy of *the great mysterious*."[4] This opening to more is key in this approach where transformative change is the goal.

3.2.2 The Personal

A plant cannot grow until the seed is sown and then has favorable conditions to germinate. Therefore, the seed and the soil enter into an indispensable relationship where new life can emerge. Similarly, the research and the researcher are not separate in that the story of the researcher is intertwined with the work. As Deah Curry and Steven Wells write, "It is the researcher's personal story or passionate interest that serves as the seed for the study."[5] This seed will be sustained only if the sacred environment supports new life in

4. Curry and Wells, *Organic Inquiry Primer*, 11; emphasis is original.
5. Curry and Wells, *Organic Inquiry Primer*, 12.

whatever form it comes forth in, and if the shape and nature of the emergent research are not dictated.

3.2.3 The Chthonic

The garden in late winter looks barren. However, a few weeks later in early spring, the hidden bulbs which have been steadily putting down roots underground emerge above the soil. They go on to flower but not always in the ways expected. The chthonic grounds the work in the physical while acknowledging the metaphysical. It implies, as Deah Curry and Steven Wells describe it, "a domain of unformed potential that can also be understood as a realm of *becoming*."[6]

This means that the researcher needs to be open to where the work might lead. Carefully made research plans may have to be altered in order to be led down an unexpected avenue. The researchers' "instincts guide the growth of the project, where they battle to overcome doubts and worries, and learn to trust the guidance they receive, and to trust themselves as disciplined knowers."[7]

3.2.4 The Numinous

Gardens seem to grow without any conscious effort. It is as if there is some hidden process which guides their development unseen by the human eye. There is a sense that there is more going on than the physical process of growth. Deah Curry and Steven Wells added this principle as a way to balance the chthonic. They describe the numinous as "the upperworld counterpart to the chthonic from which the researcher may receive inspiration, direct knowing, and other forms of intersubjective guidance."[8] This means that the researcher must be open to, as Jennifer Clements articulates it, "synchronicities, dreams, intuitions, or

6. Curry and Wells, *Organic Inquiry Primer*, 13; emphasis is original.
7. Curry and Wells, *Organic Inquiry Primer*, 13.
8. Curry and Wells, *Organic Inquiry Primer*, 15.

other manifestations of inner knowing."[9] Radical creativity can be found both in the chthonic and numinous realms so that the result is a wholistic vision of the sacred.

3.2.5 The Related

Everything in the forest is connected. The roots of a tree can extend twice the spread of the canopy. Intertwining with the soil, they come into contact with mycelium which "act as intermediaries to guarantee quick dissemination of news." This "wood wide web" helps the trees exchange news about insects, drought, and other dangers.[10] This principle in OI also acknowledges that everything is connected. Therefore, all data is seen as part of the whole and with the potential to inspire insight. Seeing all life as sacred, Deah Curry and Steven Wells state that "it is also of benefit to look beyond the human interactions, and intentionally include the relations with Spirit we will have as we follow this way of knowing."[11] This may mean linking seemingly separate sources and pieces of data so that new connections can be made.

3.2.6 The Transformative

The froth of blossoms on the pear tree in spring looks nothing like the swelled fruits which they will have become by autumn. Yet through pollination, photosynthesis, and kindly weather, they transform. Deah Curry and Steven Wells describe this principle as "a quality of difference that occurs in a shift from one set of assumptions or way of being to another, whereby an essential condition or character of a person is changed in a profound way, which may or may not be lasting."[12] The research becomes far more than information and goes to the heart of the lived

9. Curry and Wells, *Organic Inquiry Primer*, 15.
10. Wohlleben, *Hidden Life of Trees*, 10–11.
11. Curry and Wells, *Organic Inquiry Primer*, 16.
12. Curry and Wells, *Organic Inquiry Primer*, 17.

experience of the researcher. It may challenge or affirm, but it will inevitably bring about some kind of change of perspective and behavior and may even be visionary. These transformative learnings and transformative changes of the heart are not only for those carrying out the research but also for those who will eventually read the work. As the final principle in the process, it can be understood, as Deah Curry and Steven Wells note, "to refer to the process of growing a fully blossomed research project from the seed of one person's experience, a process intended to inspire others to more research on the topic or with this methodology."[13] Knowing can be achieved not only by the mind through analysis and reasoning, it can also be gained "through intuition, somatic sensation, emotion, and the elusive function we might call *felt meaningfulness* or *energetic resonance*."[14]

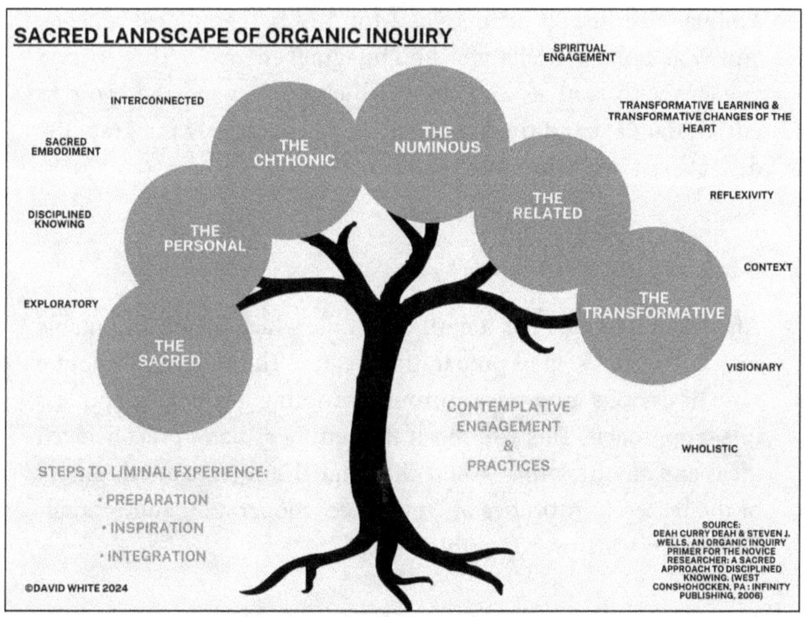

The Sacred Landscape of Organic Inquiry

13. Curry and Wells, *Organic Inquiry Primer*, 17.
14. Curry and Wells, *Organic Inquiry Primer*, 100; emphasis is original.

3.3 Three-Step Process Leading into the Liminal Realm

Transformative change is the goal of the three-step process of preparation, inspiration, and integration which may be intentional or spontaneous in nature.[15] OI puts personal experience at the heart of the process, so this method is ideally suited to topics related to psychospiritual growth. The researcher is invited to visit, as Jennifer Clements suggests, "states or sources beyond ego to gather data and then return to cognitively integrate that data into the ongoing inquiry process."[16] Jennifer Clements uses the terms "liminal" and "liminal realm" to describe a state beyond the ego that may be visited by the individual psyche to gather useful experience, a state where the ego is barely perceptible.[17] "This pattern of psychospiritual liminality is understood," Noelia Molina with insight claims, "as a form of psychological renewal and awakening of archetypal and imaginal energy."[18] This process engages with sources and states which are beyond the egoic to enrich the data and then comes back to cognitively integrate the data as part of the inquiry.

3.3.1 Preparation

After the researcher has identified a topic which would be suitable for OI, the first step of preparation begins. The ego must "adopt a state of curious ignorance" through adopting a wholistic and less linear approach. This will mean the setting aside of preconceived ideas and anything that would challenge the organic development of the research. Attitudes of "reverence, cooperation and mutuality" are the watchwords at this stage.[19]

15. Clements, "Organic Inquiry," 34.
16. Clements, "Organic Inquiry," 27.
17. Clements, "Organic Inquiry," 27.
18. Molina, "Blending Organic and Intuitive," 404.
19. Clements, "Organic Inquiry," 34.

3.3.2 Inspiration

Crossing the threshold into the liminal realm, the researcher seeks to be inspired. Setting aside the negative aspects of the ego, the researcher is in search of Spirit. "The controlling ego must endure being largely powerless," Jennifer Clements posits, "but the psyche may willfully explore this realm."[20] This stage may involve contemplative practices, paying attention to dreams, sacred embodiment of the task, or intuitive nudges in the daytime. Each researcher will draw on different sources of inspiration, but all will seek insights and some kind of meaningful encounter.

3.3.3 Integration

After preparation and inspiration comes the final step, integration. The role of the ego now comes to the fore so that it "respectfully engages with the material, examines its meaning, and is simultaneously changed by it."[21] This is where transformation and change begin to take form. The researcher may notice that linear and logical expectations are interrupted by liminal experience. This may mean that the researcher's story may have to change to accommodate this disruption so that he/she is more open to self, Spirit, and service.[22] This is where worldview comes to truly mean an integration of inner and outer worlds.

3.4 Limitations of Organic Inquiry

The limitations of this method are related to what it brings to the field of research. If everything is connected, the challenge for the researcher will be to stay focused and not treat all data equally as important. Discretion will be required so that the research maintains its concentration on essential elements.

20. Clements, "Organic Inquiry," 36.
21. Clements, "Organic Inquiry," 37.
22. Clements, "Organic Inquiry," 38.

Also, while the role of the researcher's experience is vital in this method, subjectivity and reflexivity must be balanced with objectivity and concerns for validity. This demands that the researcher has a high degree of emotional, spiritual, and psychological maturity with a healthy ego and strong intellect. Jennifer Clements names inauthenticity, narcissism, spiritual materialism, and naivete as some particular characteristics which would disrupt or jettison the integrity of the process.[23]

When it comes to validity, William Braud claims that this has to do with more than intellect alone, that the faculties of bodily wisdom, emotion and feeling responses, intuition and instinct, tacit knowing, experiential adequacy, coherence or consensus, and systematic resonances add to the strength of claims of knowing made.[24] However, this will require "discernment"[25] in order to process the data appropriately. There is also a case to be made for the researcher to bring particular personal insights to others so that they may be considered in some kind of process of "consensual validation."[26] This is to guard against the researcher being swept away by distorted thinking and to maintain the standard of disciplined knowing.

3.5 Sources of Data

The ground on which this research will be developed is my experience of growing up on a farm in horticulturally rich North County Dublin. Training and working at the National Botanic Gardens, Glasnevin, in early adulthood further deepened my relationship with the natural world through learning and working in gardens. All this experience is informed by my life as an Anglican priest and spiritual director. This research will also draw on my personal

23. Clements, "Organic Inquiry," 28.
24. Braud, "Expanded View of Validity."
25. Clements, "Organic Inquiry," 28.
26. Clements, "Organic Inquiry," 44.

garden journal, which I have kept for a number of years, as well as the research journal that accompanies this work.

However, as Jennifer Clements challenges, "Each of us lives with a narrative of who we are at the moment within our given circumstances. That story rarely reflects a reality greater than the one defined by one's ego."[27] Therefore, while engaging with autoethnographic writing, it will also be necessary to engage with contemplative practices to see if the Spirit wishes to rewrite my story as the research progresses and then to discern how this affects my interaction with the wider world. The ongoing process of spiritual accompaniment is also key here. Unsurprisingly, gardening itself will be the primary embodied contemplative practice.

OI prizes stories as a rich source of data. This research will also engage with people's stories and lived research from books and journal articles available in my personal collection and in SpIRE (Spirituality Institute for Research and Education), RCB (Representative Church Body) and SETU (South East Technological University) libraries, as well as sources available online and in other places. This data will then allow for the synthesizing of my own experience with that of others so that this interplay may allow for creative outcomes in my own context.[28]

3.6 Choice of Method

This method of inquiry has been chosen since the researcher's story is intimately interwoven with the unfolding story of the research. The progressive and revealing nature of the process resonates with the natural development at the heart of the natural world which the research will be concerned with. The method of OI, which is concerned with psychospiritual transformation, operating within the contemplative spiritual framework, will support the investigation into how a receptive engagement with gardening as a spiritual

27. Clements, "Organic Inquiry," 39.

28. Clements, "Organic Inquiry," 42.

practice allows for the emergence of a sacred environment where emotions can lead the soul deeper into the experience of more.[29]

3.7 Conclusion

While commending organic inquiry, William Braud warns that it is "demanding and challenging" and "not for the faint of heart or faint of mind."[30] This method offers many advantages over other approaches as it takes the complexity of human experience seriously. In this same vein, Larisa Bardsley writes that OI is a method

> that utilises a creative voice, valuing intuitive, emergent wisdom, a method that is self-reflexive, personally and collectively transformative, is particularly effective in exploring the human psyche and has significant heuristic value in terms of consciousness research, therapy and healing.[31]

As has been seen in this chapter, organic inquiry is a method that requires working subjectively and in partnership with Spirit to access liminal sources and ways of knowing, leading to cognitive integration, so that the process is open to the transformation of all involved.

29. For examples of other research using organic inquiry, see Ferreras, "Breastfeeding and Transpersonal Values"; Cueva, "Readers' Theatre as Cancer Education," 3–8.

30. Clements, "Organic Inquiry," 44.

31. Bardsley, "Creatively Exploring Self," 2007.

Chapter Four: **How the Soul Is Gardened**

4.1 Introduction

Gardens are spaces where people can engage with the work of allowing the emotions to lead the soul to more. The research question guiding this quest is, How can a receptive engagement with gardening as a spiritual practice allow for the emergence of a sacred environment where emotions can lead the soul deeper into the experience of more?

4.2 Gardens as Spaces Leading the Soul to More

Drawing on the Ignatian tradition in which he was steeped, Michel de Certeau stressed the "journeying" quality of the spiritual or mystical life and used this term as "both a geographical concept and a spiritual value."[1] For the seeker, there is always an intuition that there is more. This can be seen in the spiritual exercises of Ignatius of Loyola, where there is the description of the "magis," the more.[2] The impulse is to move forward, but the Ignatian tradition

1. Sheldrake, "Michel de Certeau," 209.
2. Sheldrake, *Spaces for the Sacred*, 42–43.

also speaks of rooting oneself in our desire within a time and place so that the affective side of our nature may draw us deeper.[3]

"For both the mystic and the postmodern person," as Phillip Sheldrake drawing on de Certeau explains, "'desire' expresses a certain kind of drivenness, an intensity and movement ever onwards inspired by what is *not* known, *not* possessed, *not* fixed or final."[4] There is always a tension at the heart of de Certeau's work between rootedness and homelessness, place and departure.

> He or she is a mystic who cannot stop walking and, with the certainty of what is lacking, knows of every place and object that it is not that; one cannot stay there nor be content with that. Desire creates an excess. Places are exceeded, passed, lost behind it. It makes one go further, elsewhere. It lives nowhere.[5]

However, a place, a physical location, is required to facilitate the direction of the person's development.

> A particular place—our present place—is required if there is to be a departure. . . . In order to pass from one place to another, something must be done (not only said) that affects the boundary: namely, praxis.[6]

This research is concerned with gardens and gardening. Gardens may be described as "spaces" in the sense that de Certeau means by his term "practiced places." Places have an order with elements that "are distributed in relationships of coexistence" and imply something stable.[7] Gardens then are places in that they are made up of beds of planting, hedges, paths, etc. Their design follows a particular order. Spaces, on the other hand, are dynamic and are shaped by human practices and interactions which take place there. Gardens then are spaces and "practiced places" in that they

3. Sintobin, *Trust Your Feelings*, 41–59.

4. Sheldrake, "Unending Desire," 39; emphasis is original. De Certeau, *Mystic Fable*, 299.

5. De Certeau, *Mystic Fable*, 299.

6. De Certeau, "How Is Christianity Thinkable," 151.

7. De Certeau, *Practice of Everyday Life*, 117.

are dynamic and relational. They especially become this, for example, when they are used for praxis where the soul can be nourished. The soul is, Thomas Moore reminds us, "not a thing, but a quality or dimension of experiencing life and ourselves. It has to do with depth, value, relatedness, heart and personal substance."[8] In this sacred environment, with gardening as a spiritual practice, emotions can lead the soul with its dynamic nature into the experience of more. But what is the relationship between the soul and the emotions like?

4.3 The Soul and Embodied Emotions

As a garden is made up of many parts, each required to give it dynamism and vibrancy, the soul is also composed of a combination of elements that makes the human unique, complex, and full of potential. Thomas Moore suggests that the soul "is the infinite depth of person and society comprising all the many mysterious aspects that go together to make up our identity."[9] "Who are we?" is a question many will take to their grave, reflecting the truth that becoming who we truly are is deep work and more than a lifetime's effort. We are all made of light and shadow, insight and blindness, sin and blessedness. The task before us, then, is to be willing to explore and nurture but also to prune and eradicate. The soul is gardened when we take seriously the work at hand and cultivate our souls in the same intentional ways that we grow our gardens.

Emotions animate the soul and give it color. They have neither a positive nor negative moral value. It is how they are engaged with that gives them value. The behavior which may arise from emotions can have positive outcomes or otherwise. The issue of our agency over emotions is pertinent here if we are to get to their true nature. Lisa Feldman Barrett critiques the classical view of emotion that holds that we have many emotion circuits in our brains, and each is said to cause a distinct set of changes—that

8. Moore, *Care of the Soul*, 6.

9. Moore, *Care of the Soul*, 400.

is, a fingerprint.[10] This view proposes that there is such thing as a universal experience of emotion which is innate and unaffected by culture and so is beyond our direct agency. Feldman Barrett claims that according to this classical view, emotions are "artefacts of evolution, having long ago been advantageous for survival, and are now a fixed component of our biological nature."[11] However, she contends that we have much more agency and that emotion is in fact constructed from information that the brain receives from bodily sensations and the world around us.[12]

> In every waking moment, your brain uses past experience, organized as concepts, to guide your actions and give your sensations meaning. When the concepts involved are emotion concepts, your brain constructs instances of emotion.[13]

In this view, "human beings are not at the mercy of mythical emotion circuits buried deep within animalistic parts of our highly evolved brain: we are architects of our own experience."[14] As the emotions animate and give the soul color, we are also gardeners of our own experience. How we engage with our emotions will be reflected in our choices and the decisions we make. What we imagine for the future, and work for in the present, will form the people we are becoming.

When we garden the soul, we do so as embodied emotional beings since the soul must always have a form. "An entirely independent reality known as 'soul,'" Suzanne Noffke writes, "can no more exist than a purely mechanical, unconsciously acting body can."[15] Therefore, practices can give shape to the desire for more, supported by the practiced space of the garden so that the emotions nourish and challenge the soul, which continues to journey

10. Feldman Barrett, *How Emotions Are Made*, x.
11. Feldman Barrett, *How Emotions Are Made*, xi.
12. Feldman Barrett, *How Emotions Are Made*, 30.
13. Feldman Barrett, *How Emotions Are Made*, 31.
14. Feldman Barrett, *How Emotions Are Made*, 40.
15. Noffke, "Soul," 594.

and develop. "Our 'soul' is to be found," Jürgen Moltmann encourages, "wherever we are utterly given to life, passionately interested and involved."[16] In the garden, emotions shape our souls and lead us to a more expansive experience of life.

4.4 Presentation and Discussion of Findings

Organic inquiry (OI) is a method that cultivates subjective collaboration with Spirit to tap into liminal sources and modes of understanding, ultimately resulting in cognitive and spiritual integration. This enables the entire process to be receptive to the transformation of the researcher.

Engaging with this process, within the contemplative spiritual framework, the next two sections will explore two emotions emerging from the sacred landscape of the garden. Mindful of the six principles of the OI model—sacred, personal, chthonic, numinous, related, and transformative—which are to be seen as cumulative rather than successive, the research will also involve the three-step process of preparation, inspiration, and integration. Transformative change is the goal of this process so that worldview comes to truly mean the integration of inner and outer landscapes.

The two emotions which will be focused on are love and sadness. Within the context of the garden as a "practiced place," this engagement will lead to a consideration of the embodied practices of gratitude and "everyday joy." We will see that love grows into the practice of gratitude and sadness grows into the practice of "everyday joy."

The research will engage with a variety of sources including biblical literature, the researcher's personal journal, and, since OI prizes the value of stories, published work from those engaged in gardening and the world of psychospiritual development. Underpinning the research is gardening itself, which is the primary embodied contemplative practice engaged with by the researcher.

16. Moltmann, *Is There Life After Death?*, 12.

In all of this, when attention is given reflexively to the garden and when embodied emotional practice is part of that space, threads of our own souls begin to be noticed among the flowers and trees, and birds and insects, which all leads to the potential for insight, transformation, and creative outcomes.

4.4.1 Love and the Embodied Practice of Gratitude

4.4.1.1 Introduction

Love grows into the embodied practice of gratitude. This section first explores the emotion of love and its importance in cultivating a fulfilling life. It emphasizes that love is something that needs to be nurtured and grown within oneself and that it is reciprocal and symbiotic. How love was central to early Christian communities as they navigated their identity and priorities will then be explored. The role of emotions and mood in cultivating love will then be considered, suggesting that love can become contagious when practiced, creating an atmosphere and mood of love. The threats to love are real, and the challenges that love faces, such as shame, betrayal, and withholding of affection, will then be explored. Drawing on the researcher's personal journal, the importance of listening out for the melody of love is outlined. Finally, the embodied practice of gratitude, as a way to cultivate love and embody what is valued most in life, will be examined.

4.4.1.2 Cultivating Love

Love is one of those words that can warm our hearts or send a chill down our spines. Depending on our personal experience, or the context in which the word is used, it can lead to more or bring us to a dead end. But the more we contemplate love, the more we realize that it goes to the core of everything, like the soil in a garden. Without it, we cannot have roots. Without it, we have little sense of our self-worth. Without it, we lack something life-giving and life-affirming. So, if love is so vital, can it be cultivated?

Brené Brown remarks that "love is not something we give or get; it is something that we nurture and grow."[17] It is something beyond our tangible grasp, yet it is something that we can practice in order to cultivate. Brown goes on to write that love is "a connection that can only be cultivated between two people when it exists within each one of them—we can only love others as much as we love ourselves."[18] Love is reciprocal and symbiotic. There must be something of love in the one that can respond to the love in the other. As the little seed is popped into the cold, damp earth, it would be easy to be cynical for its chances. Yet the loving earth is the very place the seed, created through God's love, needs to thrive. Soon its tender radicle bursts into the soil, heralding a fruitful future. Moisture, the warmth of the sun, and, above all, love are the ingredients for success. Love speaks to love so that love can triumph. Love leads us to our destiny.

4.4.1.3 Destined to Love

When Saint Paul planted his church in Corinth, he established love at the heart of his garden. Love was the identifier for these new Christians still trying to find their feet. These emerging communities were in the process of discerning their own identity and determining their priorities as a people who recognized the significance of Jesus' life and teaching. As N. T. Wright notes, "Paul expounds the life of love not so much as a new duty but as the Christian's new *destiny*: faith, hope and supremely love are the things that will last, the qualities which, as the fruits of the spirit, are the bridges into the new world."[19] In his view, love is at the heart of everything and always leads to more. But what does love mean to Paul?

17. Brown, *Gifts of Imperfection*, 26.
18. Brown, *Gifts of Imperfection*, 26.
19. Wright, *Paul*, 147; emphasis is original.

Paul describes in his first letter to the Corinthians what love is and what it is not. Love is patient and kind, but it is not envious, boastful, or rude. It does not insist on its own way and is not irritable or resentful. Love does not rejoice in wrongdoing but rejoices in the truth. Most importantly, "Love never ends" (1 Cor 13:8). He concludes, "And now faith, hope, and love abide, these three; and the greatest of these is love" (1 Cor 13:13). Paul uses the word *agapē* to define love, which was not a commonly used term in the first century. The more common word *erōs* was used to describe a kind of love that was "often intense, awakened and driven by the value or desirability of the object loved." The other word often used was *philia*, which is like friendship and meant "general affection for something pleasing." But these first Christians took *agapē* and filled it with "the sense of a love that confers value on an object, which may otherwise be quite unlovable."[20] They even went further, and *agapē* became a kind of atmosphere in which God and Christians live together; communicated from God, *agapē* permeated the Christian community and the individual Christian.[21] Love is our destiny when we create atmospheres where it can thrive.

4.4.1.4 Emotions, Mood, and Love

An atmosphere can be described as the external emotional tone of a place. While mood is similar, it is more of an internal emotional response. Moods may be less intense than emotions, but their effects can be "prolonged and more global."[22] They are also good indicators of how we are navigating our lives. We might be feeling optimistic, down in the dumps, or ready for anything. There are lots of things that affect mood, including the time of year. Seasonal Affective Disorder (SAD) is a type of depression that occurs in wintertime. From an evolutionary point of view, this makes sense. Maureen Gaffney explains, "Our mood system

20. Achtemeier et al., *Introducing the New Testament*, 345.
21. McKenzie, *Dictionary of the Bible*, 522.
22. Gaffney, *Flourishing*, 239.

evolved to encourage us to be less active during times of fewer resources—when there is less light, poorer vision, the days are cold and short, and sources of food are less freely available."[23] When the leaves fall off the trees, and the garden falls asleep, the workload for the gardener slows down too. The busyness is replaced by a more reflective mood, and often the mind turns to planning for the next season. Thinking of the successes of the past months, and things to adapt for the future, the gardener always looks to what is to come. There will also be choices around what to cultivate in the coming season. If the gardener chooses love, he or she may notice that this love can become "contagious."[24] Others will be affected by the love practiced by those around them. This creates both a mood and an atmosphere of love and becomes the destiny of all those in its embrace.

4.4.1.5 When Love Is Threatened

However, the challenges to love as our destiny are real. Every person suffers, and often the most painful suffering centers around love—failed love, spurned love, disappointed love. Brené Brown recognizes this and with insight observes, "Shame, blame, disrespect, betrayal, and the withholding of affection damage the roots from which love grows. Love can only survive these injuries if they are acknowledged, healed, and rare."[25] The challenge then, recognizing the mixed reality of our lived experience, is to cultivate love despite all that works to stifle it since love can often struggle to root and flourish. As bell hooks tells us,

> Everywhere we learn that love is important, and yet we are bombarded by its failure. In the realm of the political, among the religious, in our families, and in our romantic lives, we see little indication that love informs decisions, strengthens our understanding of community, or keeps us together. This bleak picture in no way alters the nature

23. Gaffney, *Flourishing*, 240.

24. Gaffney, *Flourishing*, 246–47.

25. Brown, *Gifts of Imperfection*, 26.

> of our longing. We still hope that love will prevail. We still believe in love's promise.[26]

This hopeful longing drives us on with purpose so that our deepest desire keeps us inspired and yearning to see love thrive. Love seeps into every interaction when it is allowed to grow. Transformed hearts open the future to new beginnings and to renewed understandings of the past. However, we must be mindful that the threats to love are always there and that the intentional cultivating of love is vital, which will often require courage on our part. "We cultivate love when we allow our most vulnerable and powerful selves to be deeply seen and known," Brown comments, "and when we honor the spiritual connection that grows from that offering with trust, respect, kindness, and affection."[27] For love to thrive, we must be willing to be daring, brave, and sometimes broken. By being our true selves, we allow others to reciprocate with openness in a way that does not fear judgment. Despite all the challenges, the invitation in the clamor of our emotional context is always to listen out for inklings of love.

4.4.1.6 Journal: Melody—What Am I Listening For?

Surrounded by so many plants with origins right across the globe, I have often wondered at their influence, their impact on me and my wholeness. Every garden is unique. It has its own sounds and smells and the specific blend of plants that is always particular to that place alone. It is a little like how a diversity of choristers bond to form a single choir. Separate units become a melodious unity. I am not the first to wonder whether plants sing, and if they do, do they use words? Words often get in our way, particularly when it comes to prayers and songs. The pure music is drowned out by concerns for grammar and syntax. Some Kabbalists speak of wordless melody as a way of becoming closer to God and also to the earth. Rabbi Nachman's insight has become a popular Israeli

26. hooks, *All About Love*, xxvii.

27. Brown, *Gifts of Imperfection*, 26.

song. He wrote, "Know that every shepherd has a unique melody (*nigun*) according to the grasses and the place where he herds. . . . For every grass there is a song (*shirah*) which it speaks . . . and from the song of the grasses is made the *nigun* of the shepherd."[28] The garden is already speaking to us, and from this intimacy might come our own distinct melody. But what am I listening for?

4.4.1.7 The Practice of Embodied Gratitude

By listening out for love in our lives, we cultivate an atmosphere and mood which recognizes the reality of pain and loss yet leads us on to something more. This sense of moving forward may turn our minds to how we embody what we value most through the practice of gratitude. Love seems to naturally grow into gratitude as we place our attention on all that is loving in our lives and in the world. Robert Emmons and Charles Shelton assert that "gratitude has a special place in the grammar of the moral life."[29] According to Robert Emmons and Cheryl Crumpler, it "has been conceptualized as an emotion, a virtue, a moral sentiment, a motive, a coping response, a skill, and an attitude."[30] Above all else, gratitude has the greatest value when it is embodied, when it is built into our worldview.

Gardeners are poets in the sense of the Greek *poētēs*, meaning "maker." Playfully, the poet Robert Morneau grants gratitude the color purple by "recalling the clover in a boyhood meadow" in his imagination.[31] Gardeners build gardens with such creativity. They see a landscape, or a space, and can imagine making something which does not yet exist. They make something novel through toil and dreaming—seeing beyond brambles to some kind of order and design. Color schemes and blended planting take form in the imagination before a spade is put into the ground. In order for

28. Comins, *Wild Faith*, 33.

29. Gaffney, *Flourishing*, 262.

30. Emmons, and Crumpler, "Gratitude," 56.

31. Morneau, *Color of Gratitude*, 33.

the gardener "to make," there is always a need for percolation and refinement. Vying plans excite and overwhelm at the same time. Gratitude has been described by Robert Emmons as "an interior attitude of thankfulness, regardless of life circumstances."[32] This insight suggests that life does not have to be perfect in order to feel grateful. The garden will always have weeds; that is in the nature of things. But that does not mean that nothing else can grow there. The more attention that is given to feeling grateful, the more thankfulness will bless our lives.

Contemplation allows space for embodied practices like gratitude to grow steadily at the heart of a happy life as the soul senses that it is being gardened. But it is not like the trumpeting bindweed that sprawls across hedgerows with thoughtless abandon. Instead, gratitude requires attention and the slow patient practice of noticing. It is all too easy to get wrapped up in the clamor of daily life and to miss the ordinary blessings that give life its color. The nodding daisy is overlooked for the towering redwood. And what if we cannot think of anything to be grateful for? Well then, we are not looking closely enough. The air in our lungs, the gentle breeze on our skin, the flowers in our gardens are all things we can consciously give thanks for every day. And surely there are many more things to be thankful for. This attitude opens us to the possibility of being surprised, which David Steindl-Rast describes as "more than a beginning of that fullness we call gratefulness."[33] With our feet on the warm earth, our souls can be filled with love and gratitude.

4.4.1.8 Conclusion

When we listen out for the melody of love, the response grows into the embodiment of gratitude as a practice. When Saint Paul wrote to the early church in Colossus he advised, "Above all, clothe yourselves with love, which binds everything together in

32. Emmons and Shelton, "Gratitude," 465.

33. Steindl-Rast, *Gratefulness*, 10.

perfect harmony. . . . And be thankful" (Col 3:14–15). Love and gratitude inspire a hopeful longing for our destiny which is rooted in both. When love is threatened, the challenge is to keep the promise of love before us so that we can make room for feelings of gratitude. When love is cultivated, it becomes contagious and takes root in our thankful souls. Love and the embodied practice of gratitude lead us to more.

The next section will explore how sadness grows into the embodied practice of "everyday joy."

4.4.2 Sadness and the Embodied Practice of "Everyday Joy"

4.4.2.1 Introduction

Sadness grows into the embodied practice of "everyday joy." This section first explores the unwelcome nature of sadness, but proposes that by reframing our reality and allowing untidy answers to come to the surface, we can find the life-giving roots of sadness and the potential for transformation. Next, the biblical story of Mary Magdalene at the empty tomb is examined and focuses on Jesus as empathetic gardener. Mary initially cannot see Jesus right in front of her due to her consuming sadness. However, through her devastation and loss, Mary is able to sense that there is more to come. Third, drawing on the researcher's personal journal, the juxtaposition between festivals and fasting is explored, highlighting the contrasting emotions and experiences associated with each and implying that true celebration comes from freeing oneself from negative emotions and experiences, and embracing abundance and joy. It is suggested that by cultivating a spirit of celebration and gratitude, we can see the beauty and abundance in our lives, even when faced with challenges and hardships. Finally, the researcher proposes what is articulated as the practice of "everyday joy" as a practice to cultivate and embrace joy in our daily lives. Joy is not just a fleeting feeling of happiness but a deep sense of connection and freedom that comes with virtue and wisdom.

"Everyday joy" becomes the seedbed for the quest for more and the source of sustenance for the soul's imagination to dance.

4.4.2.2 *Welcoming Sadness*

Sadness comes in many forms and, for most of us, is an unwelcome guest. However, Joseph Forgas draws on evolutionary theory and posits that "we should embrace all of our emotions, as each has an important role to play under the right circumstances."[34] Culturally we have learned to shirk from sadness as it reminds us of our incompleteness and vulnerability. We fear that sadness will darken our vision, cloud our optimism, and unsettle our confidence. Yet Joseph Forgas writes that while "much has been made of the many benefits of happiness, it's important to consider that sadness can be beneficial, too."[35] He claims that "sad people are less prone to judgmental errors, are more resistant to eye-witness distortions, are sometimes more motivated, and are more sensitive to social norms. They can act with more generosity, too."[36] Sadness, rather than being a life-limiting force, can in fact open us up to how life really is and empower us to follow our dreams with more insight and resolution.

Sadness is too often treated like an unwanted weed in the garden. When the emotion lands, the immediate desire is to root it out. It can be a little like how we used to treat dandelions. Their fluttering tooth-like petals are no longer the bane of the tidy gardener's life but remind us of the connectedness of all things. Their flowers feed bees, and their seed heads later attract finches as they flit about to feed their emerging young. Prolific weeds remind us that sometimes we just get it wrong. We need to reframe a reality before the truth emerges. But we have to give untidy answers the chance to come to the surface before we relegate them to the compost heap. "Weeds are, it is said, only plants in the wrong place.

34. Forgas, "Sadness May Be Good."
35. Forgas, "Sadness May Be Good."
36. Forgas, "Sadness May Be Good."

If you are not sure, ask a hungry bee."[37] Through contemplating sadness, we can see that its roots are life-giving and its fruits have the potential for transformation.

However, when sadness is not recognized or appreciated, it can seep into every part of us, polluting the garden with a sense of malice and impending doom, and may make us overly self-referential so that sadness becomes our only way of being. Brené Brown's research has taught her that "naming our own sadness is critical in the formation of compassion and empathy."[38] She observes that "in our saddest moments, we want to be held by or feel connected to someone who has known that same ache, even if what caused it is completely different. We don't want our sadness overlooked or diminished by someone who can't tolerate what we're feeling because they're unwilling or unable to own their own sadness."[39] Sadness has the capacity to draw us out of our interior garden so that empathy is met with receptivity, and both can blossom in the garden of relationship and collaboration.

4.4.2.3 *Jesus as Empathetic Gardener*

As Charles Spurgeon sat "in a very lovely garden, among all kinds of flowers which were blooming in delightful abundance all around," he had an experience of Jesus as gardener which changed how he saw his world.[40] His words paint a wonderful scene.

> Screening myself from the heat of the sun under the overhanging boughs of an olive, I saw palms and bananas, roses and camellias, oranges and aloes, lavender and heliotrope. The garden was full of color and beauty, perfume and fruitfulness.[41]

37. As recorded in the researcher's personal journal.
38. Brown, *Atlas of the Heart*, 108.
39. Brown, *Atlas of the Heart*, 108.
40. Spurgeon, *Supposing Him*, 7.
41. Spurgeon, *Supposing Him*, 7.

His contemplation led him to be inspired to "meditate on the church of God as a garden and to suppose the Lord Jesus to be the gardener, and then to think of what would most assuredly happen if it were so."[42] The sermon which he wrote following this epiphany draws on Mary Magdalene's mistake at the empty tomb, and there is much richness in this story.

Standing outside in the garden, Mary tries to make sense of the empty tomb. Jesus reaches out to her with great empathy and with some apposite questions leads her through her darkness. Perhaps he could recognize in Mary his own sadness, for he wept once at a tomb, that of Lazarus his friend (John 11:35).

> Jesus said to her, "Woman, why are you weeping? For whom are you looking?" Supposing him to be the gardener, she said to him, "Sir, if you have carried him away, tell me where you have laid him, and I will take him away." Jesus said to her, "Mary!" She turned and said to him in Hebrew, "Rabbouni!" (which means Teacher). (John 20:15–16)

Given the symbolic nature of much of John's Gospel, Margaret Daly-Denton makes the claim that mention of a garden would draw the original audience to think of the garden of Eden, "known to readers of the Greek scriptures as 'the Paradise of Delights.'"[43] The evangelist is insistent about the garden location of Jesus' tomb, even mentioning it twice in one sentence (John 19:41).[44] John knows that the "return to Eden" motif was widely used in Jewish writings of the late Second Temple period, which envisaged a return to love of the Torah and a concomitant recovery of wisdom—"Then humankind would return to tending the garden of the Earth as the Creator originally intended (Gen 2:15)."[45] The garden is the gateway to more.

42. Spurgeon, *Supposing Him*, 7–8.

43. Daly-Denton, *John*, 13.

44. Daly-Denton, *John*, 219.

45. Daly-Denton, *John*, 14. See also, Daly-Denton, *Caring for the Garden*, 9–12.

Mary cannot see who is right before her eyes because sadness has consumed her and narrowed her vision. But her sadness is not the end of the story. As William Barclay articulates it, "Mary is the supreme instance of one who went on loving and believing even when she could not understand; and that is the love and even the belief which in the end finds glory."[46] Through the devastation of losing Jesus, Mary is able to sense that there is more to come. The empty tomb in the garden, as Michel de Certeau affirmed, is the primary symbol of discipleship and encapsulates the onward nature of the life of faith. The invitation is always to more.[47]

4.4.2.4 *Journal: Fasting*

At first glance, festivals and fasting have little in common. Festivals speak of celebration and freedom and being in high spirits. Fasting brings to mind austerity, harshness, and loss. Yet being celebratory means to fast from dourness and drabness. To be festive means to turn our backs on scarcity and melancholy. In some monastic circles, parties are called a "gaudeamus," in other words, "we are joyful." When we fast from those things which drown our spirits, we can yield again to abundance and dance and, of course, joy. The cherry blossom petals flutter on the wind after their own quiet festive exuberance. They have celebrated and must now give way to another season. For festivals are moments in time. But could every day be festive? "What's seldom is wonderful," a wise person once said. But does this rob the everyday of potential and surprise? When our lives never see the potential for celebration, our souls lose their color. Drained of life, all we can see is what we do not have. Gratitude is buried beneath the rubble of the daily toil. We are lost, and the degree of our privation becomes our measure. The fading cherries know that there is a time for festivals and a time to let go and to move on. For every time is blessed and filled with life, if only we have the eyes to see and the will to dance.

46. Barclay, *Gospel of John*, 266.

47. Sheldrake, *World Transfigured*, 180.

4.4.2.5 The Practice of "Everyday Joy"

Joy is easily confused with happiness, and often in our daily language, we use both words interchangeably. Anne Robertson points out that the Greek word for joy is *chairo* and "was described by the ancient Greeks as the 'culmination of being' and the 'good mood of the soul.'"[48]

> Chairo is something, the ancient Greeks tell us, that is found only in God and comes with virtue and wisdom. It isn't a beginner's virtue; it comes as the culmination. They say its opposite is not sadness but fear.[49]

Joy provides the background music for the soul and, as Brené Brown notes, is "characterized by a connection with others, or with God, nature, or the universe. Joy expands our thinking and attention, and it fills us with a sense of freedom and abandon."[50] However, it is not all plain sailing. "Joy is a tricky customer," according to Harry Williams, who goes on to say,

> It seldom allows you to know where you are. It can, for instance, gate-crash into your life like an overpowering guest who dominates everything and begins to make you feel displaced. Indeed it can threaten to eat you up that your instincts of self-preservation are aroused and you begin to resist it on the plea of being overwrought. Is it pleasure or pain? You hardly know. Certainly it isn't comfort.[51]

"What a little vessel of strangeness we are," writes John Banville, "sailing through this muffled silence through the autumn dark."[52] The practice of joy then must acknowledge the sometimes bewildering complexity of our emotional lives. Joy is best cultivated in the garden of the full reality of the everyday lived experience as we are in complete empathy with ourselves. That is the reason

48. Brown, *Gifts of Imperfection*, 79–80.
49. Brown, *Gifts of Imperfection*, 80.
50. Brown, *Atlas of the Heart*, 204.
51. Williams, *Joy of God*, 9.
52. Banville, *Sea*, 53.

for this researcher describing the practice as "everyday joy." For while the experience of the emotion may seem unexpected and that it has come out of nowhere, joy is always part of the interior landscape, whether its presence is recognized or not. "Everyday joy" may be defined as something to be expected and cultivated each day, leading to further experiences such as wonder and awe. "Everyday joy" is part of that human experience which Alister McGrath has described as

> a sense of standing on the threshold of a partly glimpsed world, which seems to lie beyond the everyday reality that we inhabit, yet is somehow hinted at by what we observe around us and experience within us. Our experience of wonder somehow transcends a mere understanding of the world, seemingly enfolding us in some deeper relationship with the world we inhabit, and whatever might lie behind and beyond it.[53]

Joy forms part of the great quest for meaning. It cannot be controlled or manipulated, but its presence can be cultivated and encouraged. When "everyday joy" is embraced as an embodied practice in the garden, we are brought to the edge of our experience and sense that there is more than what is simply visible or immediately felt. Feelings of delight support the urge to play and promote creativity and skills acquisition.[54] The soul senses that it is being gardened and that a festive season is just beyond. "Gardening work," Norman Wirzba writes, "creates in us an indispensable 'imaginary' that enables us to think, feel and act in the world with greater awareness for life's complexity and depth. Gardens are the concentrated and focused places where people discover and learn about life's creativity and interdependence."[55] "Everyday joy" becomes then the seedbed for the quest for more and the source of sustenance for the soul's imagination to dance.

53. McGrath, *Great Mystery*, 107.

54. Whitehead and Eaton Whitehead, *Nourishing the Spirit*, 56.

55. Wirzba, *Food and Faith*, 37.

4.4.2.6 Conclusion

John Holdsworth is clear that the palliative care pioneer Cicely Saunder's dictum, that the antidote to death is community, is true, but he also holds that "true communities of honest sadness also have to be communities of honest joy."[56] When we embrace emotions of all kinds, we open ourselves to a complete experience of life with the possibility for, as James Whitehead and Evelyn Eaton Whitehead frame it, "surprising gains."[57] Sadness has the capacity to draw us out of our interior garden so that empathy is met with receptivity, and both can blossom in the garden of relationship and collaboration. When sadness grows into "everyday joy" and is embodied, it becomes the background music of the soul. The emotional experience can be one of wonder and excitement as something yet unfurled is noticed and loved into life. Sadness and the embodied practice of "everyday joy" lead us to more.

4.5 Unexpected Impact of the Process

This research began with the intention of exploring the role of emotions in the development of a spirituality of gardening. When the work started, the topic was approached in a detached and unemotional way so that "objective" outcomes could be achieved. However, through the process of organic inquiry, a method that requires working subjectively and in partnership with Spirit, the researcher learned that he needed to become an integral part of the process in order to access liminal sources and ways of knowing which eventually might lead to cognitive integration. This demanded a level of trust which for him was an unanticipated requirement of the research. The process of spiritual accompaniment which ran alongside the work was vital so that the challenges which emerged in this self-reflexive process could be explored more deeply. In true contemplative fashion, the researcher's inner and outer garden began to forge a strong bond. The researcher's

56. Holdsworth, *Honest Sadness*, 146–47.

57. Whitehead and Eaton Whitehead, *Shadows of the Heart*, 186.

garden journal also became very much a living document and developed into a natural part of the dialogue in the wider text. The practice of gardening itself was embodied more deeply as connections were made with the researcher's own emotional life. The final step of the three-step process into the liminal realm is integration. In light of this, the resonances which have unfurled during this current process, which have engaged body, mind, and soul, will richly inform the researcher's continuing discernment of what constitutes his own connection to more.

4.6 Strengths and Limitations of This Research

There is an impressive body of research on the role of the emotions. Therefore, any further research in this area has much material to draw from. It is clear from this research that all emotions have an important place in the growth into more. In the garden, emotions shape our souls and lead us to a more expansive experience of life. However, very little of this work has considered the garden as a suitable place for spiritual practices which takes a wholistic view of human development in general and emotional development in particular. The relevant literature available is often limited to single practices such as mindfulness.[58] The main limitation of this current research is that it has not been possible to define what "more" looks like in the lived experience. That would involve a wider and more involved process but is worthy of more attention in the future. However, there is much potential to explore how the emotions connect us to a vast garden of experience.

4.7 Further Research

Anita Phillips's book *The Garden Within* stands out as a good example of the potential for further research in this area that recognizes

58. Farrell, *RHS Gardening for Mindfulness*. Redwood, *Mindfulness in Gardening*.

the importance of emotions in psychospiritual development.[59] The garden for her is the place where she can find answers to many of the greatest questions of life through an engagement with the emotions and a close reading of the Scriptures. There is ample scope for more literature to draw on the natural processes associated with the life of a garden and also from insights drawn from gardening as an embodied contemplative practice.[60] The role of the body could be explored as the locus within the garden space of the soul's deep spiritual seeking and transformation. There may also be scope for the development of a new vocabulary drawn from both gardens and gardening which would reflect what Anne Primavesi terms our "earthiness" so that any perceived separation from the natural world could be overcome.[61] This would mean that the garden would take its place among all the great geographies of the earth in being transmuted to, as Peter London puts it, "geobiographies of our own personal journeys across time and circumstance."[62]

4.8 Conclusion

Gardens have always been places where people sought meaning. From Eden to Gethsemane, from Powerscourt to Altamont, something of these places resonated with people's souls as they yearned to connect to more. Styles of gardens have changed down the millennia, as have the lifestyles of those who created and gardened them, but what has remained constant has been the human desire for wholeness, holiness, and connection. As much as we have created and cultivated gardens, they have had their effects on us, as the life of the garden and that of the soul become intertwined.

This research has been located within a contemplative spiritual framework that supports the increase of vision, and depth of experience, and challenges any attempt to make the human

59. Phillips, *Garden Within.*

60. Watts, *Plea for Embodied Spirituality.*

61. Primavesi, *Exploring Earthiness.*

62. London, *Drawing Closer to Nature*, 202.

soul small. Contemplation gifts us the head, heart, and soul space to reflect and wonder about the vastness of human experience and the diversity of the natural world. A contemplative approach has informed organic inquiry as the research method and has challenged the researcher to go beyond the egoic and safe and to embrace the liminal and imaginal.

Emotions give color to our lives and have been at the heart of this research which sought to understand how embodied spiritual practices may find a natural locus in the garden. This research focused on the garden as a "practiced place" where emotions can lead to more by becoming embodied spiritual practices. The two specific emotions examined in this study were love and sadness, which are explored as they grow into the embodied practices of gratitude and "everyday joy," respectively. Love and gratitude inspire a longing for fulfillment rooted in hopeful promises, and their cultivation in the garden leads to a deeper connection with the self and the world. Similarly, sadness, when embodied as "everyday joy," allows for empathy and receptivity to flourish in relationships and collaborations, potentially on a daily basis.

The emotional experiences in the garden incite wonder, excitement, and connection, nurturing the soul and leading individuals onward towards discerning what embodied spiritual practices may be needed for the journey ahead. Our souls are gardened.

Epilogue

I come to my garden, my sister, my bride;
I gather my myrrh with my spice,
I eat my honeycomb with my honey,
I drink my wine with my milk.
Song 5:1

Pilgrimage is about going on a journey, but also to return to the starting point only to experience it as if for the first time. The garden can be a little like this, as there are always surprises just around the corner. Each season brings with it little treasures to behold. Just when you think you have explored every part of your outdoor space, a bulb will peep up through some abandoned soil or unexpected seedlings will germinate on the compost heap. The eyes can never be tired in a garden. The heart is regularly warmed by wonder at new and surprising things. But when the eyes are tired and the heart has been battered, it can be a strain to find the energy to have the life we want to have. The key is to be a pilgrim. Every long journey begins with a small single step. Now is the time to do little things, until the sap rises again and we feel more like ourselves. We are not machines, so our souls will not always be fine-tuned. But the garden can be the place to rest and to recover, and to return with freshness and healing in our gaze. And in all that we do, we can allow our souls to be gardened.

Bibliography

Achtemeier, Paul J., et al. *Introducing the New Testament: Its Literature and Theology*. Grand Rapids, MI: Eerdmans, 2001.

Arvay, Clemens G. *The Biophilia Effect: A Scientific and Spiritual Exploration of the Healing Bond Between Humans and Nature*. Translated by Victoria Goodrich Graham. Boulder, CO: Sounds True, 2018.

Auden, W. H., ed. *Poets of the English Language*. New York: Viking, 1950.

Banville, John. *The Sea*. New York: Vintage, 2005.

Barclay, William. *The Gospel of John: Volume Two; Chapters 8 to 21*. Revised ed. Edinburgh: Saint Andrews, 1975.

Bardsley, Larisa J. "Creatively Exploring Self: Applying Organic Inquiry, a Transpersonal and Intuitive Methodology." *The Qualitative Report* 25 (2020) 1996–2010.

Beck, Thomas E. "Gardens as a 'Third Nature': The Ancient Roots of a Renaissance Idea." *Studies in the History of Gardens and Designed Landscapes* 22 (2002) 327–34.

Bell-Williams, R., et al. "Digging Deeper: Gardening as a Way to Develop Non-Human Relationships Through Connection with Nature." *European Journal of Ecopsychology* 7 (2021) 1–18.

Benefiel, Margaret. "Epistemological Foundations for Contemplative Higher Education: Challenging the Dominant Paradigm." In *The Soul of Higher Education*, edited by Margaret Benefiel and Bo Karen Lee, 3–12. Charlotte, NC: Information Age, 2019.

Bowe, Patrick, and Keith Lamb. *A History of Gardening in Ireland*. Dublin: National Botanic Gardens, 1995.

Braud, William. "An Expanded View of Validity." In *Transpersonal Research Methods for the Social Sciences: Honoring Human Experience*, edited by William Braud and Rosemarie Anderson, 214–26. Thousand Oaks, CA: Sage, 1998.

———. "An Introduction to Organic Inquiry: Honoring the Transpersonal and Spiritual in Research Praxis." *Journal of Transpersonal Psychology* 36 (2004) 18–25.

Bridle, Susan. "Comprehensive Compassion: An Interview with Brian Swimme." *What Is Enlightenment?* 19 (2001).

Briggs, Andrew, et al. *It Keeps Me Seeking: The Invitation from Science, Philosophy, and Religion*. Oxford: Oxford University Press, 2018.

Brown, Brené. *Atlas of the Heart: Mapping Meaningful Connection and the Language of Human Experience*. London: Vermilion, 2021.

———. *The Gifts of Imperfection: Let Go of Who You Think You're Supposed to Be and Embrace Who You Are*. Center City, MN: Hazelden, 2010.

Campbell, Gordon. *Garden History: A Very Short Introduction*. Oxford: Oxford University Press, 2019.

Christie, Douglas. *The Blue Sapphire of the Mind: Notes for a Contemplative Ecology*. New York: Oxford University Press, 2013.

Clements, Jennifer. "Organic Inquiry: Toward Research in Partnership with Spirit." *Journal of Transpersonal Psychology* 36 (2004) 26–49.

Clements, Jennifer, et al. *Organic Inquiry: If Research Were Sacred*. Palo Alto, CA: Serpentine, 1998.

Comins, Mike. *A Wild Faith: Jewish Ways into Wilderness, Wilderness Ways into Judaism*. Woodstock, VT: Jewish Lights, 2007.

Cooper, David E. *A Philosophy of Gardens*. Oxford: Oxford University Press, 2006.

Cueva, Melany. "Readers' Theatre as Cancer Education: An Organic Inquiry in Alaska Awakening Possibilities in a Living Spiral of Understanding." *Journal of Cancer Education* 25 (2010) 3–8.

Curry, Deah, and Steven J. Wells. *An Organic Inquiry Primer for the Novice Researcher: A Sacred Approach to Disciplined Knowing*. West Conshohocken, PA: Infinity, 2006.

Daly-Denton, Margaret. *Caring for the Garden of the Earth: A 5-Part Bible Study*. Edited by Ginnie Kennerley. Dublin: Biblical Association for the Church of Ireland, 2020.

———. *John: Supposing Him to Be the Gardener*. An Earth Bible Commentary. New York: Bloomsbury, 2019.

Davis, Jody L., et al. "Interdependence with the Environment: Commitment, Interconnectedness, and Environmental Behavior." *Journal of Environmental Psychology* 29 (2009) 173–80.

De Certeau, Michel. "How Is Christianity Thinkable Today?" In *The Postmodern God*, edited by Graham Ward, 135–58. Oxford: Blackwell, 1997.

———. *The Mystic Fable*. Translated by Michael B. Smith. Chicago: University of Chicago Press, 1992.

———. *The Practice of Everyday Life*. Translated by Steven F. Rendall. Berkeley: University of California Press, 1984.

Delio, Ilia. *The Unbearable Wholeness of Being: God Evolution and the Power of Love*. New York: Orbis, 2013.

Dillard, Anne. *Pilgrim at Tinker Creek*. Norwich: Canterbury, 2022.

Egan, Keith J. "Contemplation." In *The New SCM Dictionary of Christian Spirituality*, edited by Philip Sheldrake, 211–13. London: SCM, 2005.

Emmons, R. A., and C. A. Crumpler. "Gratitude as a Human Strength: Appraising the Evidence." *Journal of Social and Clinical Psychology* 19 (2000) 56–69.

Emmons, R. A., and C. M. Shelton. "Gratitude and the Science of Positive Psychology." In *Handbook of Positive Psychology*, edited by C. R. Snyder and S. J. Lopez, 459–71. Oxford: Oxford University Press, 2002.

Farrell, Holly. *RHS Gardening for Mindfulness*. London: Mitchell Beazley, 2020.

Feehan, John. *The Singing Heart of the World: Creation, Evolution and Faith*. Dublin: Columba, 2010.

Feldman Barrett, Lisa. *How Emotions Are Made: The Secret Life of the Brain*. London: Pan, 2018.

Ferreras, Olga. "Breastfeeding and Transpersonal Values: An Organic Inquiry." *Consciousness, Spirituality and Transpersonal Psychology* 4 (2023) 64–79.

Forgas, Joseph P. "Four Ways Sadness May Be Good for You." *Greater Good Magazine*, June 4, 2014. https://greatergood.berkeley.edu/article/item/four_ways_sadness_may_be_good_for_you.

Frohlich, Mary. "Spirit, Spirituality, and Contemplative Method." *Mysterion*: 12 (2019) 129–39.

———. "Spiritual Discipline, Discipline of Spirituality: Revisiting Questions of Definition and Method." *Spiritus* 1 (2001) 65–78.

Gaffney, Maureen. *Flourishing: How to Achieve a Deeper Sense of Well-Being, Meaning and Purpose - Even When Facing Adversity*. London: Penguin Life, 2011.

Gunnlaugson, Olen, et al., eds. *Contemplative Learning and Inquiry Across Disciplines*. New York: SUNY, 2014.

Guroian, Vigen. *Inheriting Paradise: Meditations on Gardening*. London: Darton, Longman and Todd, 2001.

Hide, Kerrie. *Love's Oneing: A Book About Contemplation*. London: Austin Macauley, 2022.

Holdsworth, John. *Honest Sadness: Lament in a Pandemic Age*. Durham: Sacristy, 2021.

hooks, bell. *All About Love: New Visions*. New York: Harper Perennial, 2000.

Hughes, Gerard W. *God in All Things*. London: Hodder & Stoughton, 2003.

Jalics, Franz. *The Contemplative Way: Quietly Savoring God's Presence*. Translated by Matthias Altrichter. New York: Paulist, 2011.

Jordan, Martin. "Ecotherapy as Psychotherapy - Towards an Ecopsychotherapy." In *Ecotherapy: Theory, Research and Practice*, edited by Martin Jordan and Joe Hinds, 58–69. London: Palgrave, 2016.

Keane, Marc. *Japanese Garden Design*. North Clarendon: Tuttle, 1996.

Koay, Way Inn, and Denise Dillon. "Community Gardening: Stress, Well-Being, and Resilience Potentials." *International Journal Environmental Research and Public Health* 17 (2020) 6740. https://doi.org/10.3390/ijerph17186740.

Lane, Belden C. *The Solace of Fierce Landscapes: Exploring Desert and Mountain Spirituality*. New York: Oxford University Press, 1998.

Latour, Bruno. "Ecological Mutation and Christian Cosmology." In *If We Lose the Earth, We Lose Our Souls*, translated by Catherine Porter and Sam Ferguson, 19–35. Cambridge, UK: Polity, 2024.

London, Peter. *Drawing Closer to Nature: Making Art in Dialogue with the Natural World*. Boston: Shambhala, 2003.

Mac Coitir, Niall. *Ireland's Wild Plants: Myths, Legends and Folklore*. Cork: Collins, 2015.

Magan, Manchán. *Listen to the Land Speak: A Journey into the Wisdom of What Lies Beneath Us*. Dublin: Gill, 2022.

McGrath, Alister. *The Great Mystery: Science, God and the Human Quest for Meaning*. London: Hodder & Stoughton, 2018.

McKenzie, John L. *Dictionary of the Bible*. London: Chapman, 1965.

Millen, Lydia. *Evergreen: Discover the Joy in Every Season*. London: Orion Spring, 2023.

Miller, Lisa. *The Awakened Brain: The Psychology of Spirituality*. London: Penguin, 2022.

Miller, Mara. *The Garden as Art*. Albany: State University of New York Press, 1993.

Molina, Noelia. "Blending Organic and Intuitive Research Methods: Spiritual Transformation." *Mysterion* 12 (2019) 403–10.

Moltmann, Jürgen. *Is There Life After Death?* Milwaukee, WI: Marquette University Press, 1998.

Moore, Thomas. *Care of the Soul: A Guide for Cultivating Depth and Sacredness in Everyday Life*. New York: Walker, 1992.

Morneau, Robert. *The Color of Gratitude: And Other Spiritual Surprises*. New York: Orbis, 2009.

Morris, Paul, and Deborah Sawyer, eds. *A Walk in the Garden: Biblical, Iconographical and Literary Images of Eden*. Sheffield: Sheffield Academic, 1992.

Murray, Anja. *Wild Embrace: Connecting to the Wonder of Ireland's Natural World*. Dublin: Hachette Ireland, 2023.

Naydler, Jeremy. *Gardening as a Sacred Art*. Edinburgh: Floris, 2011.

Noffke, Suzanne. "Soul." In *The New SCM Dictionary of Christian Spirituality*, edited by Philip Sheldrake, 592–94. London: SCM, 2005.

O'Brien, Dan, ed. *Gardening: Philosophy for Everyone*. Chichester: Blackwell, 2010.

Parker, Blake. *A Forest of Ideas: Ramblings in Interpretative Frameworks*. Bloomington: Trafford, 2014.

Phillips, Anita. *The Garden Within: Where the War with Your Emotions Ends and Your Most Powerful Life Begins*. Nashville: Nelson, 2023.

Primavesi, Anne. *Exploring Earthiness: The Reality and Perception of Being Human Today*. Eugene, OR: Cascade, 2013.

Redfern, Martin. *The Earth: A Very Short Introduction*. Oxford: Oxford University Press, 2003.

Redwood, Ark. *Mindfulness in Gardening: Meditations on Growing and Nature*. Brighton: Leaping Hare, 2023.

Reynolds, Mary. *The Garden Awakening: Designs to Nurture Our Land and Ourselves*. Cambridge, UK: Green, 2016.

Roche, Arthur. *The Gardens of God*. Washington, DC: Word on Fire, 2023.

Rohr, Richard. *Everything Belongs: The Gift of Contemplative Prayer*. New York: Crossroad, 2014.

———. *Immortal Diamond: The Search for Our True Self*. London: SPCK, 2013.

Rolf, Veronica Mary. *An Explorer's Guide to Julian of Norwich*. Downers Grove, IL: IVP Academic, 2018.

Romanyshyn, Robert. *The Wounded Researcher: Research with Soul in Mind*. New Orleans, LA: Spring Journal, 2007.

Sanna, Ellyn. *All Shall Be Well: A Modern-Language Version of the Revelation of Julian of Norwich*. New York: Anamchara, 2018.

Sheldrake, Philip. "Michel de Certeau: Spirituality and the Practice of Everyday Life." *Spiritus* 12 (2012) 207–16.

———, ed. *The New SCM Dictionary of Christian Spirituality*. London: SCM, 2005.

———. *Spaces for the Sacred: Place, Memory and Identity*. London: SCM, 2001.

———. "Unending Desire: De Certeau's 'Mystics.'" *The Way Supplement* 102 (2001) 38–48.

———. *A World Transfigured: The Mystical Journey*. Collegeville, MN: Liturgical Press Academic, 2022.

Simard, Suzanne. *Finding the Mother Tree: Uncovering the Wisdom and Intelligence of the Forest*. London: Penguin, 2022.

Sintobin, Nikolaas. *Trust Your Feelings: Learning How to Make Choices with Ignatius of Loyola*. Dublin: Messenger, 2022.

Soga, Masashi, et al. "Gardening Is Beneficial for Health: A Meta-Analysis." *Preventive Medicine Reports* 5 (2017) 92–99.

Spurgeon, Charles H. *Supposing Him to Be the Gardener: A Sermon Delivered on Lord's Day Morning, December 31st, 1882, at the Metropolitan Tabernacle, Newington*. Updated to modern language by Charles J. Doe. Minneapolis: Curiosmith, 2014.

Steindl-Rast, David. *Gratefulness, the Heart of Prayer: An Approach to Life in Fullness*. New York: Paulist, 1984.

Sternberg, Esther. *Healing Spaces: The Science of Place and Well-being*. Cambridge, MA: Belknap, 2009.

Stuart-Smith, Sue. *The Well Gardened Mind: Rediscovering Nature in the Modern World*. London: William Collins, 2020.

Utsler, David. *Paul Ricoeur and Environmental* Philosophy. Lanham, MD: Lexington, 2024.

Varela, Francisco J., and Jonathan Shear. "First-Person Methodologies: What, Why, How?" *Journal of Consciousness Studies* 6.2–3 (1999) 1–14.

Versluis, Arthur. *Awakening the Contemplative Spirit: Writing, Gardening and the Inner Life*. St. Paul, MN: New Grail, 2004.

Wall Kimmerer, Robin. *Braiding Sweetgrass: Indigenous Wisdom, Scientific Knowledge and the Teachings of Plants*. London: Penguin, 2020.

Watts, Fraser. *A Plea for Embodied Spirituality: The Role of the Body in Religion*. London: SCM, 2021.

Whitehead, James D., and Evelyn Eaton Whitehead. *Nourishing the Spirit: The Healing Emotions of Wonder, Joy, Compassion and Joy*. New York: Orbis, 2012.

———. *Shadows of the Heart: A Spirituality of the Negative Emotions*. New York: Crossroad, 1994.

Williams, H. A. *The Joy of God*. London: Mitchell Beazley, 1979.

Wirzba, Norman. *Food and Faith: A Theology of Eating*. New York: Cambridge University Press, 2011.

Wohlleben, Peter. *The Hidden Life of Trees: What They Feel, How They Communicate; Discoveries from a Secret World*. Translated by Jane Billinghurst. London: Willima Collins, 2015.

Wright, N. T. *Paul: In Fresh Perspective*. Minneapolis: Fortress, 2009.

www.ingramcontent.com/pod-product-compliance
Lightning Source LLC
LaVergne TN
LVHW020655100826
845148LV00012B/2501

9798385247196